T·A·K·E C·O·N·T·R·O·

HEALTH DEFEN

preserve and improve your natural good health

Books supplying expert information and practical guidance to help YOU take control

Titles published so far include

ALCOHOLISM
an insight into the addictive mind
Dr Clive Graymore

·

STROKE!
a self help manual for relatives and carers
Dr R. M. Youngson

·

SCHIZOPHRENIA
a fresh approach
Gwen Howe

·

FERTILITY
a comprehensive guide to natural family planning
Dr Elizabeth Clubb and Jane Knight SRN

·

DRUG ABUSE
the truth about today's drug scene
Tony Blaze-Gosden

HEALTH DEFENCE

Preserve and Improve Your Natural Good Health

Dr Caroline Shreeve MB, BS (Lond)

A DAVID & CHARLES health book

British Library Cataloguing in Publication Data

Shreeve, Dr Caroline
    Health Defence: preserve and improve
    your natural good health.—(Take control).
    1. Health
    I. Title   II. Series
    613   RA776

    ISBN 0-7153-9031-7

Typeset by Typesetters (Birmingham) Ltd,
Smethwick, West Midlands
Printed in Great Britain
by Billings Limited, Worcester
for David & Charles Publishers plc
Brunel House   Newton Abbot   Devon

Distributed in the United States by
Sterling Publishing Co. Inc, 2 Park Avenue, New York, NY 10016

Contents

Foreword

In writing *Health Defence*, I have had two main objectives. The first has been to provide a simple explanation of infection and the workings of the body's defence systems from the orthodox point of view, juxtaposed with the holistic view of how and why infectious (and other) diseases develop. The second has been to find as many meeting points as possible between the conventional and the 'alternative' medical viewpoints, in order to formulate an effective plan for strengthening our resistance to illnesses generally.

As time progresses – though the gap between the orthodox and certain alternatives remains very noticeable – it becomes a little easier to reconcile the scientifically founded discipline of the orthodox medical profession, with the philosophically and intuitively based beliefs of alternative therapists. Neither the attitude that demands 'scientific evidence' for the value of every therapeutic approach, regardless of obvious benefits to patients, nor the ingenuous attitude that denies the value of deductive reasoning, can hope to provide the final answer to this or any other health problem.

Ultimately, it can only be through mutual acceptance – and respect for – one another's approaches to health problems, that orthodox practitioners and alternative therapists will learn all that the 'other' side has to offer. At that point, the alternatives will become truly 'complementary' to standard medical practice. Perhaps, looking beyond the next decade or so, which I see as a 'growing together' period, certain aspects of orthodox medicine will in turn become 'complementary' to a number of alternative therapies that are currently establishing themselves as valid medical systems.

There is a great deal of value to be learned from the holistic approach. Its fundamental concept is one of balance and harmony, and it sees the life force or vitality of living creatures as a state of dynamic equilibrium between internal forces and the external environment. The naturopathic view is the one I have chosen as widely representative of holism generally. And when one examines it closely – 'without prejudice', to borrow a popular legal phrase – it does not differ as markedly as might be supposed from the conventional one.

Orthodox practitioners are being made more and more aware of the need for living organisms to be in harmony with the world about them. The threats to human, animal and plant life when the surrounding environment is alien, are dealt with in detail in the first chapter. Similarly, the necessity for internal harmony was, as I describe later in the same chapter, made clear for all time by one of the greatest of orthodox practitioners, Professor Claude Bernard.

In naturopathic terms, good health is the sum of three inner drives in perfect balance with one another. These are described as structural, biochemical and psychological or emotional. Orthodox doctors may not express the components of the health equation in precisely similar terms, yet we are becoming more and more conscious of the significant roles mental and emotional equilibrium play in a person's overall well-being. (The necessity for structural integrity and biochemical balance have never been doubted!)

Not only are an increasing number of diseases being found to be due, at least in part, to stress, but the necessity for 'lightness of spirit' and spiritual welfare are also being given credence. This is one of the chief reasons why diversional therapy has come into being, and why it is attracting more and more interest from those who care for cancer patients.

Regarding treatment, while naturopathic and some other alternative practitioners abhor the use of drugs (except in extreme circumstances), which they see as weakening our natural defences, orthodox treatment regimens often include forms of therapy that are essentially naturopathic. Many medical practitioners realise the benefits of fasting, live juices and a wholesome, high-raw diet, as well as the crucial need for relaxation and exercise. And some are happy to prescribe herbal remedies, homoeopathic medicines and biochemic tissue salts (Chapter 9). If they are skilled in neither plant medicine nor the principles of homoeopathy, an increasing number are taking the trouble to become acquainted with alternative practitioners in their area and refer patients to them. Certainly, many now recommend air ionisers largely for the treatment of respiratory complaints, and it is interesting to note that the novel idea of laughter therapy (Chapter 9) is becoming an established form of therapy in hospitals in the United States.

Lastly, I have tried to provide a clear idea of our first- and second-line defence mechanisms, in particular the immune defence system. While it is relatively simple to describe and understand how first-line resistance works (ie, the protective function of the skin, mucous membranes, stomach acid and so on), and how the reticulo-endothelial system functions, the immune defence reaction is a great deal more complex. Understanding its structure and action, however, is essential to a comprehensive understanding of how the resistances of the body can be strengthened against disease. So I have described it as simply as possible, hoping that in so doing, I have made the basic concept of immune defence comprehensible to those for whom it is new, while not irritating readers with a medical or scientific background.

Certainly, when I was at medical school, lectures on immunology remained unpopular all the time they were delivered by a brilliant research fellow who had difficulty in conveying knowledge in a comprehensible way. When he left to carry on research elsewhere and was replaced by a new lecturer who was vividly aware of how offputtingly complicated immunology can seem to beginners, many of us began not only to understand the principles of immune defence activity, but even to enjoy the topic.

It now only remains for me to thank the authors to whose books I have referred for information in writing this book. These include too many to name individually, but particular thanks must be expressed to Roger Newman Turner, author of *Naturopathic Medicine* (Thorsons Publishers); Brian Inglis and Ruth West, authors of *The Alternative Health Guide* (Michael Joseph); Leon Chaitow, who wrote *Amino Acids In Therapy* (Thorsons); and Leslie Kenton, who wrote *Ageless Ageing* (Century Arrow). My thanks are due, too, to medical practitioners both orthodox and alternative, who have given me the benefit of their knowledge and expressed their interest in this book.

1 Our Health Under Threat

Our health is constantly under siege from the world around us. When asked to think about this for a moment, most people agree, and point to obvious environmental hazards such as industrial accidents, accidents encountered in travel, atmospheric and environmental pollution, radiation, and bacterial and viral infections. These are certainly part of the problem but it does not end there. In fact, it is only the tip of the iceberg.

Human life on this planet has always been beset by dangers. Cave man had to contend with wild animals, extreme weather conditions, the paucity of plant food after a bad season, and attacks from neighbouring cavemen bored with hunting bears. Look briefly at the ensuing pages in the history of civilisation, and each age will be found remarkable for the problems Man has had to face and overcome, for the mistakes he has made, and for what he has learned.

Over the centuries, we have come to understand a very great deal about the world in which we live. So much do we know about our environment, in fact, regarding both how and why it functions, that we might well expect life to be both simpler and less hazardous than it once was. The truth of the matter, however, is very different. What we appear to have done, is to have exchanged one set of environmental problems for another.

One commonly hears middle-aged and elderly people say that life is not what it used to be when they were young. Rather than listening to their point of view, it is sometimes tempting to ignore their negative comments and remind them of the great advances that have been made since the beginning of the century. Technology, mathematics, physics and engineering have advanced to the point at which interplanetary travel is practically within our grasp. Medicine and surgery are in the process of mastering the problems of successful *in vitro* (test-tube) fertilisation, heart, liver and lung transplantation, and effective cancer treatment.

The advent of the microchip has revolutionised electronic engineering to the point at which cheap, cheerful and highly efficient computers have become standard school learning equipment, and desk-top publishing accessible to many modern companies.

ENVIRONMENTAL HAZARDS

Despite these impressive achievements, however, and the undeniable improvements in many aspects of our standard of living, our environment poses a greater threat to life than ever before. At least cavedwellers could, in the main, *see* their adversaries, and learn by a process of trial and error, as well as deductive thinking, how best to overcome them. What does the average man or woman (or doctor, company chairman or politician, come to that) *really* know about the long-term effects of atmospheric radiation, or of the increased mercury contamination of the seas from which our fish are caught?

There are some who claim that we have lost more than we have gained. Those who feel nostalgic about life as it was between the world wars and earlier, have some valid criticisms to make about the quality of life today, and the ways in which our health is being slowly and silently eroded. It is foolhardy to refuse to consider them.

Food and drink, it seems, tasted better then. In particular, our attention is drawn to basic, daily dietary items such as freshly baked bread, cheese, butter, milk and other dairy products, eggs, red meat and poultry, fresh fruit and vegetables. Peoples' sense of taste gradually loses its youthful sensitivity as they get older, and it is easy to dismiss this belief as an effect of the ageing process. On the other hand, it seems likely that mass-produced food today does lack the flavour remembered from bygone years. You have only to eat a piece of sliced, plastic-wrapped bread made from denatured, bleached flour, followed by a hunk of crusty wholemeal bread fresh from the oven, to realise why people are insisting on 'real' food, and many manufacturers are beginning to supply the demand.

The underlying problem is that many of us have forgotten how food ought to taste. Food manufacturers have seized upon our need for fast, easily prepared food in plentiful supply and have taken the opportunity to produce just what we appear to want, at ever-increasing speed and in ever-increasing quantities. Rapid mass production means that the dairy products, red meat and poultry in our shops are derived from artificially reared animals doctored with hormones and antibiotics.

Eggs (apart from the relatively few free-range ones) come from 'egg factory' battery hens, that are never permitted to feel the sunlight on their feathers, nor to breathe fresh air and stretch out their cramped limbs. Fruit and vegetables are forced into 'season' under unnatural conditions with the aid of synthetic chemicals.

In addition, most commercially prepared food and drink products are given longer shelf-lives by the addition of chemical preservatives, and a more 'attractive' appearance and flavour, by the addition of laboratory-produced colours and flavours. Maurice Hanssen's book *E For Additives* (Thorsons Publishers, 1985) played an important role in drawing our attention to just what we do swallow without realising it.

Older people level further criticisms against life in the 'eighties, besides the ever-rising cost of living, the unemployment problem, and the frenetic pace of life generally. These include poorer weather, overcrowding on the roads, an increased level of noise, a rise in the crime rate and the dangers of pollution. It is debatable whether our summers really are shorter, colder and wetter than they were in the early part of the century – human recollection tends to retain pleasant memories and repress unpleasant ones – but many people are convinced that this is in fact the case.

A meteorological report in the latter half of the catastrophically wet summer of '86, went to some pains to stress that our climate has undergone no real changes for the worse over the past decades. One wonders whether, like the Player Queen in *Hamlet*, the authorities do protest too much.

No one can deny the overcrowding on the roads. The problem of commuting to and from work has assumed such titanic proportions that specific periods of rush-hour traffic into and out of major cities are no longer recognised. The traffic flow – or rather, lack of flow – is constant throughout the day. In addition, the nervous wear and tear experienced by daily commuters contributes heavily to the increased incidence of stress-related complaints. Familiar examples include complaints such as raised blood pressure, peptic ulceration, migraine attacks and spastic colon. A further environmental hazard stemming from grossly congested roads is an increase in the atmospheric pollution problem.

Life is noisier than it was fifty years ago. The main factors causing this have been the growth in the size of population, the increased pace at which life is lived, the continuous and growing need for both public and private transport, and the greater availability of televisions, radios, and stereo cassette players. All of these apart from televisions now come in readily portable sizes and shapes so that those addicted to them can use them wherever they happen to be. Many people play cassette and radio music at full volume while walking along the street or travelling by public transport. We seem to be powerless to stop the ever-mounting tide of decibels.

There is some evidence that constant subjection to a high noise level blunts our finely tuned sense of hearing and may even cause damage to the delicate hearing mechanism, resulting in a degree of deafness. In addition, unwelcome, jarring sound, whether it is a next-door neighbour's hi-fi or the incessant roar of main-road traffic, engenders a degree of stress that can have serious health consequences in certain people.

There are ample figures to prove that the crime rate has increased over the past few decades. This growth in violent crimes includes murder, robbery with violence, mugging attacks upon the elderly, frail and disabled, and the use of offensive weapons including knives and firearms. Rape and the sexual abuse of children pose an obvious threat to health, life and sanity. In some ways, this growth in crime can be identified as a segment in a vicious circle in which other environmental health hazards play a causative role. These include social factors such as overcrowding, the stress of life in urban areas, unemployment, boredom, and the easy availability of drugs and alcohol. Others include the influence of the media and racial disharmony.

Many child-health experts believe that poor nutritional standards, including vitamin and mineral deficiencies, inadequate physical exercise and relaxation, and too little exposure to fresh air and sunlight, are partly to blame for disruptive and violent tendencies in children and adolescents. A deficiency of zinc, and of certain essential fatty acids, combined with a junk-food diet, has been strongly linked with hyperactivity. The synthetic yellow food colourant tartrazine in particular seems to worsen the condition. Lead toxicity, too, has been associated both with hyperactivity and with impaired intellectual performance.

Large-scale pollution includes radioactive fallout, the only too familiar dangers of nuclear-power production, the ineffective disposal of nuclear and other toxic waste material, acid rain, and contamination of the air with petrol fumes, tobacco smoke, industrial toxins and crop insecticides. Apart from the uncalculated but harmful effects that exposure to toxins is having upon the human race, it is tempting to speculate that atmospheric pollution may well be partly contributing to the poorer climatic conditions older people are certain exist.

An additional factor which needs to be taken into account is the extremely serious effect of deforestation upon the earth's atmosphere. Green foliage takes in carbon dioxide gas from the atmosphere and gives off oxygen during daylight hours, reversing the procedure during the night. Destroying vast areas of tree and plant life inevitably causes changes to occur in the quality of the air we breathe and upon weather conditions.

In the name of progress, therefore, we appear to have sacrificed many things of value. Among the most important are plenty of open space, tranquillity, and a more leisurely, reflective lifestyle. Just as bad as their loss is the fact that we may have made this planet a more dangerous place in which to live and rear our children. The human race appears to be bent on self-destruction. No wonder predictions are cast yearly that the end of the world is nigh!

NATURAL BALANCE

Before we become irremediably depressed, though, it is essential to remember Nature's inborn tendency to correct imbalance and restore harmony. Profound changes have occurred throughout the ages in the climate of the earth and the geological structure of its outer crust. We as a race have perpetrated horrific and indefensible assaults upon our planet's natural resources. Nevertheless, when left to her own devices, Nature generally manages to balance the books in favour of life on earth, and the continued existence of our planet in the surrounding universe.

I should like to comment here upon the personification of natural forces by 'Nature' spelled with a capital 'N'. This is deplored by some people as unattractively coy and unscientific. My personal idea of nature is of an infinitely powerful life force capable of perpetuating the healthy life of plants, animals and humankind on this earth. Providing, that is, that the very foundations of Nature are not tampered with in ways that will inevitably upset the harmony of the laws governing the life process.

In forcing animals and plants to grow and multiply under artificial conditions, disseminating toxic waste throughout our atmosphere, soil, rivers and seas, destroying vast areas of vegetation for personal gain, and seeking for better and more effective means of committing genocide, I believe we are committing crimes whose heavy penalty we will inevitably have to pay at a later date.

A balanced interplay of constituent parts is fundamental to the functioning of any organism. This includes the universe as whole, as well as planet earth. It is vital, for instance, that the oxygen concentration in the air remains at its usual level of around twenty per cent. The problems that would ensue should this level suddenly drop, will be familiar to anyone who has suddenly found themselves at an unusually high altitude where the air pressure is markedly reduced.

The oxygen level in the atmosphere depends, in turn, upon the healthy growth of an adequate amount of plant life. Other constituents such as water vapour content depend upon evaporation from the surfaces of the oceans and rivers, overall temperature, and height above sea level.

Man also depends completely upon plant and animal life for his food. Both in turn require appropriate and stable conditions in which to thrive and reproduce, and the necessary factors include clean air, sunshine, an uncontaminated supply of fresh water, warmth and protection from the elements.

MACROCOSM AND MICROCOSM_____

The ancient Greeks used the term 'macrocosm' to represent the whole world, or universe at large, all of whose constituent parts were interdependent. The secret of the universe's existence lay in balance, each part co-operating with others in a state of harmonious interplay, and each contributing in its own way a vital factor to universal equilibrium. With the genius of intellect typical of early Greek thought, they then conceived humankind as a 'microcosm' (little universe or world), seeing in people a model or epitome of the universe in which they lived.

The philosophers were able to form this image of human life because they noted the parallels that exist between the inter-dependence of the various components of the world at large and the interplay of a human being's constituent parts. Although there was little knowledge (despite a great deal of theory) about the detailed structure and function of the human form, the ancient philosophers noted the significance of each part to the whole, and of the dependence of the whole organism's health upon the well-being and integrity of its various structural units.

Numerous examples drawn from present-day knowledge of anatomy and physiology can be found to illustrate this point. The satisfactory passage of the blood around the body, for example, is dependent upon the pumping action of the heart, and upon the smoothness and elasticity of the walls of the arteries, as well as upon the interiors of the great veins. Equally vital to the process of circulation is the massaging effect of the leg muscles which, by their contracting, squeezing action, encourage blood to flow upwards towards the heart against the pull of gravity. The negative pressure within the chest when breath is drawn also helps the blood – again against the earth's gravitational pull – to travel up the great vein (inferior vena cava), draining the lower part of the body, and to enter the heart.

The function of the heart, in turn, is governed by both the central and the autonomic nervous system, as well as by the hormones and other chemical messengers secreted by the endocrine glands according to need into the blood.

The eternal truth of the macrocosm/microcosm philosophy was

summed up in the great precept underlying hermetic magic. This message, 'As above, so below', was engraved before the beginning of time upon the emerald tablet of Hermes Trismegistus, the thrice-great one and the herald of the gods.

The sages of the ancient Greek world recognised a further vital fact of which scientific modern man is only gradually becoming aware. That is, that the true well-being of humankind depends upon the harmonious integration, not only of interdependent anatomical parts, but also of body, mind and spirit. The cells of our various organs, including those of our immune defence system, are indisputably influenced by our state of mental health and of our spiritual attunement or disharmony.

HOLISM

In their turn, our mind and spirit are affected for good or ill by our physical condition. This way of considering man as a 'whole' organism, with a tripartite nature whose integral parts are equally important and interdependent, is known as 'holism'. A true holistic approach to healing, or to strengthening a bodily system should, therefore, pay as much attention to our mental and spiritual states, as to the biochemical functioning of the systems concerned. Even at the purely physical level, the system or part of the body in question, has to be viewed as an anatomical, physiological and biochemical part of the whole person, intimately connected by both structure and function with every other part.

Consider for a moment the standard treatment for asthma sufferers. Depending upon the severity of the condition, patients treated by orthodox doctors might be given a drug such as sodium cromoglycate, which stabilises mast cells and helps to prevent further attacks. In addition, they may be prescribed a cough elixir and, most likely, drugs known as bronchodilators which relax the tight bronchial air tubes. A sudden, acute attack may result in a rush to the casualty department of a hospital, where a life-saving injection of adrenaline or aminophylline will probably be administered. These drugs act swiftly and directly upon the severely constricted air tubes, permitting the patient to breathe normally again. Long-term treatment may include steroid drugs, and possibly intermittent courses of antibiotics for recurrent chest infections.

In all these cases, it is the asthma symptoms which are receiving attention, rather than the patient as a whole. It is quite possible that emotional stress at home, work or school is largely to blame. Delving into the patient's psychological state often reveals an underlying predisposition to asthma coupled with emotional problems acting as trigger factors. Bringing these to light is often more therapeutic than unchallenged drug therapy, especially if relaxation exercises are prescribed in conjunction with effective psychotherapy.

This is not to deny the role that drugs for asthma – and many other conditions – play in saving life and improving its quality. One has only to consider pain-killing compounds, anaesthetic agents, and antibiotic and anti-viral drugs to realise the fallacy of decrying drug treatment as harmful, just because this has become a fashionable thing to do. At the same time, it is important to realise the great advantage that the holistic approach has over the allopathic (orthodox), which tends to focus its diagnostic and therapeutic skill solely upon the part of the body most obviously affected. Orthodox doctors are becoming more aware of the need to think of the patient as a whole being, with psychological and emotional needs besides the more simple physical ones.

Doctors with sufficient time *are* likely to ask about emotional stress and possible sources of mental strain, besides carrying out other, physical tests such as blood investigations and skin tests. The same applies when patients suffering from other stress-related problems are being treated. All the same, many doctors have neither the time nor the inclination to take lengthy case histories when it is quicker and usually effective to write out a prescription. To counterbalance this problem, doctors at the other end of the spectrum of approach, are likely nowadays to suggest a course of autogenics or yoga, as a means of learning to relax properly.

Not much credence, however, is as yet attached by allopathic practitioners to a person's state of spiritual balance. The very notion sounds thoroughly nebulous and unscientific, and attracts little real interest. An exception to this generalisation, however, is beginning to make an appearance among medical teams working with terminally ill patients. A film entitled 'Invitation to the Ballet' was recently made on behalf of the pharmaceutical company, Lederle Laboratories, who are currently sponsoring visits from the Royal Ballet Company of Covent Garden, London, to cancer patients in hospitals and hospices, as a form of 'diversional therapy.'

A nursing officer interviewed about the beneficial effects upon patients of having something to which to look forward, stated:

> A great deal of our time in hospital is spent caring for patients' physical needs. But there is another dimension to the patient's life that we have to care for too, the spiritual or psychological.
>
> So we really have to think in terms of all sorts of avenues that we can explore, to help them in when they are at a difficult period of their illness.

A general though vague feeling of being out of sorts with the cosmos at large and the rest of the human race in particular is a common symptom of spiritual unrest. It is very probably as capable in its own way of predisposing a person to asthma attacks, as is psychological stress or an allergy to house dust.

HOW WE ACHIEVE BALANCED HEALTH____

In this book we will be looking at a particular means we have at our disposal for maintaining our bodies in a state of balanced health and equilibrium. The system concerned, the immune defence system (IDS) is a complex set of interrelated cellular and biochemical mechanisms whose collective aim is protection from infectious illnesses. This system is vitally important to us, for invasion by bacteria and viruses is capable under certain conditions of causing a very wide variety of disease processes and frequently death. The letters of the very serious disease AIDS stand for 'acquired immune deficiency syndrome', and a vital aspect of the illness is injury to and collapse of the immune defence mechanisms.

We will look, firstly, at what exactly the IDS comprises. We will then consider ways of strengthening and energising it at a cellular level, and examine appropriate psychological and spiritual techniques for boosting its total resources.

The human form of IDS is highly sophisticated, and has no

counterpart among the less advanced creatures such as the single-celled animals (protozoa) and the invertebrates (animals without backbones). No trace of such a system appeared, in fact, until the primitive marine vertebrates came into being some four hundred million years ago[1].

It was not until a mere two hundred and fifty million years ago that a system comparable to ours appeared in the more highly evolved sharks. Since then, the IDS has grown in both complexity and refinement, and can be recognised in reptiles, birds and mammals.

Immune defence, however, is only one of many different means by which we maintain our internal systems in working order. It was the great French physiologist Claude Bernard (1813–78), professor of physiology at the Sorbonne in Paris and of medicine at the College de France, who first described the concept of our internal environment, which he termed 'le milieu intérieur'. It has been said of Bernard that, had Nobel prizes existed in his day, he could hardly have been awarded fewer than four!

Bernard's self-professed aim was to establish a firm scientific basis as the foundation from which future medical knowledge could develop. Like Descartes before him, he assumed nothing, but drew his deductions from proven scientific fact. Unlike Descartes, he followed a line of enquiry only as far as experimental results led him, testing and retesting the results in a variety of ways and drawing fresh conclusions from these.

His many discoveries include the digestive function of the pancreas, the control of blood vessels by nerves, the transport of oxygen by red blood cells, a number of facts about the functioning of the brain and spinal cord, and much information about the glands and the kidneys.

The concept of le milieu intérieur, however, is more closely associated with the name of its inventor than all of Claude Bernard's other discoveries. In contrast to our external surroundings, which constantly change, he pointed out that our internal environment is maintained in a state of constant steadiness, despite the fact that delicate physiological mechanisms are readily affected by changing external factors such as temperature, water supply, available nourishment, the oxygen available in the atmosphere and so on.

---

1. Bricklin, M. The Practical Encyclopedia of Natural Healing Rodale Press, page 333

He recognised that the independence of the human organism (and of other mammals) within this context is due to the interplay of a number of delicately balanced mechanisms. Their purpose is to keep the inner domain – the sea of blood and tissue fluid bathing the cells of the body – in a balanced state within a very narrow set of parameters most suited to the cellular function of the organism as a whole.

HOMOEOSTASIS

Bernard termed this state of inner balance 'homoeostasis', derived from the Greek words *homoeo* (similar) and *stasis* (a standing still). He pointed out the regulatory mechanisms responsible for achieving and maintaining it. The skin, for instance, plays a vital role in the control of body temperature, by flushing and perspiring in hot weather and constricting its blood vessels away from contact with the outside air when the temperature falls. The kidneys are essential to life because they play a major part in regulating the body's water balance and the acidity of the blood, and in removing toxic waste. The liver, in turn, plays a most important part in detoxifying and helping to excrete harmful substances, as well as supplying glucose into the bloodstream commensurate with our changing needs. The circulatory system transports around the body both the breakdown products of metabolism so that they can be excreted, and the oxygen and nutrients the cells need for growth and repair.

This brings us to two other types of physiological activity, without which all these measures to regulate the internal biochemical environment would be pointless. The first of these is the ability to carry out repair operations. We do of course take it for granted that bruises fade, that abrasions develop scabs and heal, that fractures mend, that torn muscles and ligaments knit together again and that scar tissue forms after a serious burn. You have only to think of the condition most of us would by now have reached, were our body cells not capable of constant renewal, to realise what a vital role this process has in maintaining life and health.

Within this context, we should not forget the life-saving activity of the blood-clotting mechanism. So strong is Nature's urge to maintain a state of homoeostasis within the living organism, that the blood of humans and of most of the higher mammals is imbued with an extraordinarily complex system for inhibiting harmful bleeding. This system involves the interplay of the tiny particles in the blood called the platelets, as well as that of numerous chemical factors, which produce between them the tendrils of fibrin which form the basis of the clot. Under normal conditions, this mechanism is stimulated into action whenever injury causes blood to be shed, either from the surface of the body or internally.

Examples of the deficient working of this system are seen in patients with a reduced number of platelets in their blood (a condition called thrombocytopenia), and in people suffering from haemophilia or Christmas disease. All three conditions cause abnormal bleeding to occur. Thrombocytopenia is usually a temporary condition occuring as a symptom of a more generalised disease, and responds to the treatment of the underlying condition.

The blood of both haemophiliacs and Christmas disease patients lacks a clotting factor vital to the clotting mechanism as a whole. Transfusions of blood plasma containing the relevant factor is the only treatment available if fatal internal or external bleeding is to be avoided.

The other important mechanism which protects us from serious injury and internal disruption involves our ability to deal with environmental hazards. This is known as our first-line defence mechanism, a collective term for the various protective means our bodies use against invasion by harmful external agents. These include noxious chemicals, the toxins present in food and drink, and pathogens (ie, pathogenic or harmful organisms) such as bacteria, viruses, fungal spores, single-celled parasites, and the more complex parasitic invaders.

We will look in further detail at the anti-invasive techniques our bodies employ in the next chapter. From there, we will go on to look at our secondary protective mechanisms which are called into operation once invasion has occurred, and at the important role our immune defence system plays in this capacity.

2 How Our Natural Defences Become Weakened

The sayings 'Everything has its price' or, alternatively, 'Nothing is ever free' are clichés. They are, however, as is so often the case with clichés, perfectly true. We saw during the first chapter of this book that much that is good and beneficial to mankind has been sacrificed in the name of progress. That that progress has been of immense value to millions of members of the human race, and to certain members of its animal and plant life, is beyond reasonable doubt. It remains a fact, though, that many of the advances we have made in a wide variety of fields, perhaps especially that of the medical sciences, have turned out to be two-edged swords.

Consideration of infectious illnesses and their control provides an interesting case in point. Certainly, effective and safe sanitation and drainage facilities, the aseptic surgical techniques which have replaced the earlier antiseptic methods, and the sophisticated technology upon which modern isolation units are based, are unquestionably beneficial. But a number of orthodox medical practices carry with them indisputable stings in their tails, and the practitioners of conventional medicine are often among the first to admit it.

Once 'microbes' (bacteria, fungi, protozoa and viruses) had been discovered and finally accepted as the cause of contagious diseases rather than a product of them, doctors, surgeons and research workers breathed a sigh of relief. There were, after all, many reasons for them to do so. Awareness of a major aspect of the nature of infection was the first effective weapon of combat ever available against the suffering caused by, and the tremendous fear engendered by, infectious illness.

The devastating toll that so many forms of contagious diseases had taken of human life, in some cases, such as the plague, wiping out entire village communities in one fell swoop, seemed capable of redress. Part of the redress started to be put into practice with the advent both of vaccination techniques, and of antibacterial drugs.

VACCINATION: THE CONTROVERSY_____

Besides the hopefully permanent success that vaccination against smallpox has had in wiping out this life-threatening infection, victories have been gained with this protective technique in many other fields. Immunisation methods have been strikingly effective against polio, diphtheria and tuberculosis, as well as against a multiplicity of tropical illnesses.

Cholera, yellow fever, typhoid, infective hepatitis need hold no serious danger for holidaymakers today, regardless of where they choose to spend their vacation, while intrepid travellers to really remote areas can rest assured of protection against rabies should they have the misfortune to be bitten by an infected animal.

A further great benefit from the science of vaccination has been the development of a Rubella vaccine using the live but freeze-dried viruses in an attenuated form. This is an advance of great magnitude, offering protection against the harm German measles can do to the unborn child. It is given to women who have never suffered from the illness and therefore have no immunity against it in the form of ready-made antibodies.

About the overall advisability of immunisation, however, the most immense controversy rages. The resulting schism splits not only orthodox doctors and the practitioners of alternative or complementary medicine, but also different members of each of these two main groups. Vaccination, like many other forms of treatment, has a capacity for doing harm, just as it has for doing good. Immunisation against pertussis (whooping cough) is a case in point.

Because of 500 cases of brain damage from whooping cough

vaccine reported to the English health authorities, uptake of the vaccine dropped by sixty per cent. Within a year, the incidence of the disease had risen by a factor of 9 to 50,000 cases, resulting in nine deaths from the infection in England. Simon Mills, a herbalist well known in England, expressed aspects of both sides of the argument in a sensitive, objectively written article which appeared in the *Journal of Alternative Medicine* in February 1984.

This feature is worth quoting extensively from, for the writer has some vitally interesting points to make about the immune defence system as part of the overall protective mechanisms afforded by the body.

Simon Mills agrees with all the points to be made in favour of the practice of immunisation, and emphasises that siding with those who oppose vaccination is to assume a very heavy responsibility. Nevertheless, he says:

> Blind reliance on an exogenous stimulation of the immune system for protection against infectious diseases leads attention away from those factors predisposing or precipitating the disease in the first place. It complies with the current mythology that 'germs' are like bullets, striking down their victims in a random fashion, malevolent agents that merely need to be eliminated for disease to be eradicated.

Mr Mills goes on to outline the wider ecological perspective – that 'germs' have as many potential survival problems as other living organisms with which they co-exist, and that they can only thrive when they meet congenial conditions. Our defence mechanisms normally provide perfectly adequate protection against bacterial, fungal and viral invasion with which we are actually constantly threatened. The more constructive approach is to examine individual infectious illness and discover ways of enhancing the protective powers normally evoked against invasion by the pathogen concerned.

Mr Mills provides the example of enteric infections, such as bacterial food poisoning, typhoid, dysentery and cholera. The organisms responsible for these infections, he says, are unlikely to survive exposure to the highly acid conditions of normal gastric secretions. (It is interesting that hot spices and bitter herbs increase the output of protective gastric secretions.)

Of universal interest and application, are the ubiquitous common cold and 'flu, from which certain individuals never seem to suffer, regardless of the frequency with which they are exposed to contagious sufferers. Such people, says Mr Mills, seem capable of maintaining resistance to a wide spectrum of rhinoviruses causing these illnesses, presumably by denying them adequate nutrition and shelter on the mucous membrane lining of the respiratory tract.

The approach of herbal medicine, in contrast to that of immunisation or of symptomatic relief adopted by orthodox practitioners, is that of boosting the natural defence mechanisms of the patient by specific herbal remedies. This can prove a highly effective way of treating colds and 'flu, and can also improve resistance to them.

The argument against immunisation is a two-pronged one. At the public health level, it would appear far more sensible to spend government funds on improved nutritional, housing and social standards, 'widely agreed to be by far the most significant factors in the aetiology of infectious illnesses'. And at a personal level, since each human being is an individual, it is more reasonable to deal with individual weaknesses in resistance as and when these appear, rather than relying upon an arbitrary intervention.

Mr Mills does not condemn the practice of vaccination per se, and concedes that it may well be the treatment of choice in instances where the individuals concerned could not be expected to adopt all the positive measures necessary to enhance their own innate resistance mechanisms. Nevertheless, at least in the ideal situation, boosting natural resistance from a choice of possible strategies seems by far the best approach.

It is also important to remember that immunisation can have serious side effects in certain individuals. Vaccinations against viral infections, for example the common cold and influenza, are derived from viruses bred on embryo chick cells, and can evoke a serious allergic response in an individual sensitive to eggs, chicken, chicken feathers and so on. Moreover, some of the vaccinations induce in susceptible people very unpleasant symptoms similar to those of the illness against which the vaccination is directed. Many jabs, for example, cause pain and swelling local to the innoculation site, as well as a mild feverish illness accompanied by swollen glands, malaise and headache. Some people react to yellow fever vaccination in this way, while others may find that cholera or typhoid vaccine causes the same effects.

Among the possible alternative strategies are included the homoeopathic alternative to immunisation, and the approach of naturopathic medicine. We will examine the former of these in Chapter 9, and the latter, later on in the present chapter. At this point, it is pertinent to look at the other great advance in medical science – the birth of antibiotic and antiviral drugs – and discover what, if anything, is to be said in their disfavour.

ANTIBIOTICS What are the real dangers?____

Within this section, we are considering the rationale and the implications of treating infectious illnesses, not only with antibiotic (antibacterial) drugs, but also with antiviral agents, anti-fungal drugs, and drugs directed against protozoal infestation. We are scrutinising the whole approach of attacking the invading organisms as though they really were 'malevolent agents that merely need to be eliminated for disease to be eradicated'.

Against the immediate rationale of treating infectious illnesses with drugs that kill the causative pathogens, very little can be said. A patient with an ear infection, for example, is often in a great deal of pain as the inflammatory process gets under way, and there is a risk of both ruptured ear drum and/or of infection of the mastoid bone behind the ear, if a rampant infection remains untreated.

Likewise, bacterial pneumonia and severe bronchitis, kidney infections, an infected wound or severely burned area, or an abscess in or near a vital organ, are just a handful of examples of conditions in which radical and intensive antibacterial drug therapy is not only wise but essential.

Where one can justifiably question the wisdom of prescribing antibacterial and similar drugs is in instances such as recurrent laryngitis (frequently due to a viral infection or nervous strain), recurrent cystitis (where there is often no evidence of a bacterial cause to be found), or head colds and 'flu, which are of viral origin and generally unaffected by antibiotic agents.

Not only are antibiotic drugs frequently ineffective (as are many useful tools when used for the wrong job), they can be literally hazardous when used incorrectly. This often means 'too frequently', as well as for the wrong conditions, and one of the most serious outcomes of their misuse is the spread of resistant strains of bacteria. Many organisms are capable of 'mutation', that is, altering their genetic coding during the course of reproduction, in such a way that their offspring are able to resist bacterial drugs aimed at their destruction.

Thus, a particular strain of Staphylococcal bacteria may succumb in a perfectly satisfactory manner to a particular type of antibiotic. If this antibiotic is used again and again, however, for trivial purposes, the Staphylococci 'learn' to alter their metabolic requirements accordingly. The next time the patient receives a prescription for 'the usual' penicillin, he discovers that it is not nearly as effective as before. Back he goes to his doctor, puzzled at the lack of response.

Tests performed on relevant pathological specimens (such as sputum in the case of a chest infection, or pus from a wound that is slow to heal), will reveal during the course of the 'sensitivity' tests, that resistance has taken place. The bacteria concerned now grow and thrive quite happily on a standard jelly-broth plate used in bacteriology laboratories for the purpose, in the closest proximity with an absorbent paper disc impregnated with the very antibiotic that proved fatal to it on past occasions.

The implications of the resistance phenomenon are far-reaching, and very serious in the case of patients who are continuously suffering from one type of infection or another. One example is a patient suffering from lung damage and recurrent bronchitis (see Chapter 3). Another is that of a patient with serious kidney disease on renal dialysis, who often succumbs to infections of one type or another. A third is that of the operation site that will not heal, despite every measure being taken to encourage it to do so.

Such individuals are bound to receive life-saving antibiotics at fairly frequent intervals, and this certainly does not constitute an example of overprescribing. But many unnecessary cases of bacterial antibiotic resistance *do* arise, simply because so many people – patients and doctors – think that it is far better to ask for/ prescribe an antibiotic 'to be on the safe side'.

In addition to the development of resistance, and the difficulty doctors and bacteriologists have in finding a suitable and effective antibiotic for a patient, there is the problem of 'superinfection' (see Chapter 3), due to the killing off of helpful and useful bacterial types in a particular area.

Another problem encountered by patients on antibiotics is the side-effects. Antibiotics are as capable as any other class of drug of causing unwanted symptoms, and a number are renowned for 'upsetting' those who have to take them, or at least are obliged to find out for the first time that they are unsuited to them.

A number of the antibiotics commonly prescribed for the treatment of cystitis are particularly likely to cause nausea and vomiting. Many people are allergic to certain forms of penicillin, although this is less frequent these days than it was when the early penicillins were introduced, because the penicillin forms are purer and carefully synthesised in the laboratory to suit human metabolism. The allergy symptoms can fit anywhere into a whole spectrum of severity, from a mild skin rash to what is called an 'anaphylactic' reaction in which the tongue swells, the throat constricts, and immediate resuscitatory measures are required to save life.

Other common antibiotic side effects include gastro-intestinal upset (especially diarrhoea), headaches, drowsiness, loss of appetite, interference with the efficacy of the birth-control pill, and possible (although unlikely) effects upon the unborn baby of a woman who takes them during the first trimester (first thirteen weeks) of pregnancy.

OUR STATE OF DEFENCE

Quite apart from the problems of over-prescribing and of side-effects, it is gradually becoming more and more apparent to orthodox doctors and other medical experts that 'killing the responsible organism' is inadequate in itself and can prove injurious. Although we tend to think of infections only when we or someone in our family succumbs to an infectious illness, or when newspaper reports warn us of a coming 'flu or measles epidemic, our defence mechanisms are in fact on 'alert call' twenty-four hours a day, every day of the year.

It is no coincidence that we remain infection-free most of the time, and it would be extremely naïve of us to assume otherwise. The fact is that our first- and second-line defence mechanisms are waging a continual battle – for the most part, successfully – against the invasion by pathogenic organisms of our *milieu intérieur*.

Paying critical, scientific attention to the body's own resistance mechanism is now appealing to many physicians and alternative practitioners as the most sensible approach when dealing with infectious diseases. To give the majority of alternative practitioners their well-deserved due, this has been their view for many decades and, in the case of the older established ones, for many centuries.

There are, after all, two possible approaches to the problem of winning a military battle. A general in charge of an army closeted with his troops inside a well-defended fortress which is about to be besieged, can aim at victory by weakening and killing the opposing ranks. Alternatively, by so strengthening his own military resources, onslaughts by the opposing numbers can be easily and capably dealt with.

If he adopts the first of these strategies, he runs the risk of losing many of his own men and weakening his side considerably. Strengthening his resources of military power, however, is just as effective a method of keeping the enemy at bay, and he runs less risk of having his own forces decimated in the process. He can either call in parachute reinforcements from the nearest military base, and supply his men with extra arms and comrades. Alternatively (or in addition), the general can retain his original number of troops and so strengthen their fighting power with extra food, and better living conditions, that they become practically invincible. This latter method is the philosophy upon which the alternative approach to the treatment of infectious illnesses is based.

OUR INTERIOR TERRAIN

In modern times, Claude Bernard (see Chapter 1) was the first orthodox doctor to advocate the way of thinking outlined above. He maintained that the body's homeostatic mechanisms were potentially capable of defending it against invasion by pathogenic organisms. When the balance of *le milieu intérieur* is upset, however, (by factors such as chronic malnutrition, excessive stress, prolonged fatigue or environmental toxins), the defence mechanisms break down.

Louis Pasteur's reaction to Bernard's philosophy impresses itself upon both memory and imagination, when one considers the role he played in demonstrating the significance of bacterial organisms and their role in infectious diseases. He said when he was dying: 'Bernard is right. The germ *is* nothing: the terrain is everything'. By the terrain, Pasteur meant the body and the condition of its innate defence mechanisms. To use the above analogy, in fact, he referred to the enemy action being of relatively little importance, and to the strength of the 'fortified garrison' (the body), as all important.

It is now widely accepted that pathogens do not simply 'cause' an infection because they happen to be transmitted to a human host, but that infectious illnesses represent a breakdown in the body's defence mechanisms. Twentieth-century research workers and doctors have certainly not reverted to the nineteenth-century view that infectious illnesses produce pathogens, rather than the other way round (ie, the theory of 'spontaneous generation'). But in 1942, J. E. R. MacDonagh, former Hunterian Professor of the Royal College of Surgeons in London, suggested in a letter to *The Times* that viruses should be regarded, not as a cause of infectious illnesses but as its consequence. That is, the consequence of a breakdown in the body's powers of resistance. Viruses, in fact, are difficult organisms with which to come to terms, both with respect to their physical and biochemical structure, and to their behaviour.

Before we go on to look in detail at exactly how our defence mechanisms, specifically our immune defence system, become depleted, it is worth noting a theory about the spread of infection that ties in closely with holism (see Chapter 1).

Pheromones

How infection spreads, and how epidemics occur are no longer believed to have simple explanations. Various theories have been propounded to explain them and the one pertinent to the holistic concept is that of Doctor Lewis Thomas, author of *The Lives of a Cell* and President of the Sloane-Kettering Memorial Center in New York. He has suggested that epidemics may be spread by free-floating scent molecules called pheromones. These, he says, may either deplete our innate defence resources, or stimulate the organisms with which we normally maintain a harmless contact, into vigorous pathogenic activity.

The existence of pheromones has long been established and they are believed, among other activities, to explain in part the mystery of the intense sexual attraction that so often binds two people unexpectedly and for no obviously apparent reason. Should Dr Lewis Thomas's explanation be the correct one, with respect to the spread of infection during an epidemic, no reason has yet been suggested for why the airborne pheromones should suddenly act in this injurious way.

The authors of the account of his theories from which I am quoting[2] say: '. . . the most plausible explanation is that in some way they transmit what might be described as a psychic infection, of the kind that quite commonly breaks out in schools and is put down to hysteria. Perhaps hysteria is pheromone-activated'.

If you have ever been caught up in a crowd in which mass hysteria breaks out (the author's experience was at Victoria station in London during a Friday afternoon rush hour, when a bomb scare was suddenly announced over the loudspeaker system and everyone was urged to vacate the place as rapidly as possible), then you may well have picked up what amounts to an actual 'scent' of fear. This is experienced through one's nose and within one's frontal sinuses in the forehead, although no odour of any kind is detectable.

Animals, in particular dogs, can 'sense' danger, fear, anger and affection. The dog's sense of smell is thousands of times keener than that of a human being. It could well be that our various emotions and states of mind are all represented by different varieties of pheromones, detectable as an odour to dogs and, when extremely marked, as an 'odd feeling' to sensitive humans.

The idea that pheromones may spread epidemics 'as a psychic infection' is exciting because it forms a vital link with the idea that our psychological and emotional states play very important parts in our overall balance of health. Holistic theory holds the physical, psychological and spiritual aspects of man's nature to be of equal importance, and entirely interdependent and inter-reactive. As acceptance of holism grows, so more and more attention is paid to

2. Inglis, B. and Wet, R. The Alternative Health Guide Michael Joseph, London, page 312

how our states of mind and emotions affect our susceptibility to disease.

YOUR MOODS AND INFECTION_____

Chronic stress and anxiety, for example, are believed to play important parts in the generation of certain cancers, heart and circulatory disease, gastrointestinal problems and autoimmune conditions. Of greater relevance to us here, negative states of mind, especially anger and depression, are thought to deplete our defence systems and make us more prone to infections. Scientists working at the American National Institute of Health have recently uncovered substantial proof of this.

They believe that the defensive white blood cells react strongly to signals of mood change that occur in the brain, and are released into the bloodstream as different types of chemical molecule. Part of the reason for this belief is observation of the significant changes in activity that the white blood cells undergo in response to mood-altering drugs such as tranquillisers. There is already evidence that a number of brain chemicals do affect our ability to withstand infection. This is further, objective proof of the holistic belief that our health is governed at all times by the way our bodies, minds and emotions interact.

NATUROPATHIC TREATMENT: RESTORING HARMONY_____

The principles of holism are evident in most forms of alternative medicine, but none exemplifies them better than naturopathic medicine. This system of medicine, also known as 'natural medicine' or naturopathy, is founded upon three tenets. Firstly, the body has innate self-healing power due to the presence of the life force within it, and to its natural instincts for self-preservation. We can equate the 'life force' with energy, well-being and vitality, and the 'natural instincts for self-preservation' with the homoeostatic mechanisms which maintain our internal environments in a state of balanced equilibrium.

The second building block of naturopathy is that the appearance of symptoms of an illness are proof that the life force is at work and is trying to re-establish equilibrium. Health is a state of dynamic equilibrium maintained between man's mechanical structure, bio-chemical makeup and psychological or emotional attributes. Disease, on the other hand, is a state of disharmony that results from instability of one of the three factors. The energy for the system in dynamic equilibrium is derived from the life force itself, the concept of which is fundamental to naturopathic theory and practice.

Thirdly, the holistic principle itself appears as a fundamental aspect of naturopathy, in that naturopathic doctors consider body, mind and spirit when a patient complains of an illness. This has much in common with the second tenet cited above, and em-phasises the need to consider the patient as a whole person (hence the name 'holism'), instead of, say, an interesting gastrointestinal or respiratory problem. It is the aim of naturopathic medicine to get to the root cause of the problem, and never simply to treat the symptoms which the patient is complaining about.

Restoring harmony

This may sound odd at first, for it is the 'symptoms' of which we complain when we seek treatment, and they are clearly indicative that something is amiss. Naturopaths, however, regard many symptoms, for example, the production of phlegm from the chest, a fever, signs of inflammation, as the body's attempts to eliminate toxins that have accumulated as a result of an 'unnatural' lifestyle.

By this, they mean inadequate and inappropriate diet, lack of exercise and fresh air, exposure to prolonged stress and the effects of environmental toxins upon health. For this reason, many of their treatment methods are aimed in the first instance at promoting the excretory activities of the body manifesting as symptoms, rather than simply trying to repress or abolish them.

In many ways, therefore, the naturopathic approach to disease and treatment is diametrically opposed to the orthodox approach. Conventional doctors do not talk about diseases as the result of unbalanced life force, and neither do they regard symptoms as proof of toxin excretion. Nevertheless, many naturopathic forms of treatment, such as fasting, the adoption of a wholefood diet, exercise, relaxation and help with emotional problems are prescribed for their value and innate common sense, by orthodox practitioners. Health is the product of harmony between bio-chemical, structural and psychological factors.

Biochemical upset
This is recognised primarily in the fluids of the body, such as the blood, urine, vaginal secretions, bile, gastric juice and tissue fluid. The many manifestations of this type of upset are caused by inadequate or harmful diet, inadequate excretion of waste products by the skin, lungs, kidneys, liver, bowel, or by poor circulation.

Mechanical problems
Our skeletal components (bones, tendons, muscles, ligaments, cartilage, joints) can cause disharmony throughout the body when the posture is bad, the spine held crookedly, the muscles contracted with chronic anxiety and stress, and the muscles and joints misused or under-exercised.

Psychological factors
Psychological and emotional problems can cause internal dis-harmony when stress and emotionally traumatic events are not equalised by relaxation and positive thinking. Chronic anxiety and depression can become established, and these can lead to a multiplicity of illnesses, including increased susceptibility to infection.

NATUROPATHY AND INFECTION_____

In Chapters 5–8 we will be looking at ways in which changes in lifestyle, diet and relaxation can strengthen the body's defence mechanism in general, and the immune defence system in particular. The methods to be discussed have indisputably beneficial effects, and reduce the risks of contracting infections in a striking way. They also coincide, in many instances, with the naturopathic approach.

Naturopathy is an art rather than an exact science whose effects have been qualified and quantified by the type of controlled trials used by conventional medical research. There are many reasons why this is so, and space does not allow the examination of the subject in any detail. Suffice it to say, though, that naturopathic treatment is beneficial to many patients, and that there are, as we mentioned above, many meeting points between naturopathic and conventional medical treatment methods.

For this reason, it seems a good idea to prelude our discussion of natural-defence-system strengthening techniques with a brief resumé of the naturopathic view of the body's second-line defence mechanisms and of infectious illness as a whole. From necessity, though, the spotlight of attention will have to be focused upon only a small aspect of naturopathic philosophy and must perforce omit a very great deal of both relevance and interest. The naturopathic view of disease as summarised above, can be amplified as follows.

The disturbance of normal equilibrium (ie, an upset in the body's state of homoeostasis), causes disease. This disturbance is brought about by two sets of causal factors, prenatal and postnatal. Prenatal factors include genetic makeup predetermined at conception, and influence upon the baby during its development in the womb. Among the latter, must be mentioned the lifestyle of the mother during pregnancy, including what she eats, whether she is a smoker or nonsmoker, how much alcohol she drinks, the degree of stress in her life, and her emotional and mental well-being.

The postnatal causal factors include physical trauma, mental stress, inadequate nutrition and chemical pollution from the atmosphere and food, as well as disturbances arising *within* the body, such as abnormal bacterial flora in the intestines, toxic foci such as bad teeth or recurrent abscesses, and harmful stimuli such as an allergic response.

The unbalanced equilibrium resulting from these disturbing factors depletes the individual's state of cellular vitality, a condition known in naturopathy as 'mesotrophy'. Mesotrophic changes are due to a slow accumulation of waste products of metabolism (for example, carbon dioxide as excreted by the lungs, urea as excreted by the kidneys), and environmental toxins (such as synthetic additives present in processed convenience foods).

The removal of these injurious toxins depends upon adequate powers of excretion through lungs, kidneys, skin, large bowel and so on. For this to occur, nutrition has to provide all the necessary factors required by human physiological processes. In addition, the natural resilience of the body has to remain unhampered by slumping posture, strained joints, ligaments and tendons, or permanently tense muscles. Finally, all the body tissues have not only to receive adequate supplies of freshly oxygenated blood but have also to be drained effectively of their used blood, stale tissue fluid (lymph) and excretory products.

When these requisite factors are not present, the toxins that accumulate in the tissues and organs of the body provide a suitable environment for the growth and multiplication of pathogenic organisms. For this reason, bacteria, viruses, fungi and other pathogens are the *secondary* cause of infectious diseases, rather than their *primary* cause.

Most symptoms of acute disease (for example, diarrhoea, vomiting, catarrh, cough, sneezing, the appearance of a rash, fever) are an outward sign of the body's striving to return to a state of balance (homoeostasis). They are the positive signs of a vital response and need not be feared.

NATUROPATHY AND DEFENCE SYSTEMS___

Naturopathic theory recognises the vital parts played by our second-line defence systems (the reticulo-endothelial system (RES) and the immune defence systems), regarding their purposes primarily in terms of the neutralisation and elimination of impurities. It maintains that when the body's excretory functions are impaired, the RES becomes more active than usual in an effort to cope.

Sooner or later, though, it fails to keep pace with the gathering toxic material, and the general standard of the individual's health declines (ie, he is in a state of mesotrophy) although not as yet experiencing any overt symptoms. The toxic substances that accumulate in this way, are derived not only from poorly excreted waste material but also from exogenous toxins such as those already mentioned. An authority on the subject of naturopathy, Roger Newman Turner, includes in the list of such substances, both drugs and vaccines administered for the prevention of infections[3].

It can be seen from this account, how vital the balanced homoeostatic state of the internal environment is to the naturo-

3. Newman Turner, R. *Naturopathic Medicine* Thorsons Publishers, Wellingborough, UK, page 38

pathic interpretation both of chronic diseases that take a long time to produce symptoms, and of acute infectious illnesses. The holistic view of naturopaths, that the homoeostatic breakdown which necessarily precedes successful pathogenic invasion is due to emotional, biochemical or mechanical stress, will underlie much of the restorative and strengthening techniques discussed in later chapters.

3 Understanding Our Bodies' Defences

We saw in Chapter 1 that our bodily organs and systems constantly interact to keep our internal environment (Claude Bernard's *milieu intérieur*) in a state of balance. In health, this is effectively maintained despite the changing nature of our surroundings and the demands made upon our bodies' resources. We also have active means of defence at our disposal to help us cope with specific environmental hazards, such as foreign bodies, noxious gases, toxic substances and pathogens. This chapter, and the next, explains how our defence systems work, so that when we come to look at the practical things we can do to help ourselves later in the book, you will already have a basic understanding of the dynamics of illness and health. If you would prefer to start reading about self-help, turn to Chapter 5, and read up on the background information presented here when you feel you need to.

Our defence mechanisms can be divided into two groups – those in our first line of defence against the invasion of external agents, and those that come into force once invasion has taken place.

FIRST-LINE DEFENCE

The skin

It is easy to forget that the skin is a body organ. This term is usually reserved for more distinct anatomical units such the kidney, brain or liver. Nevertheless, the skin has a clearly defined structure and variety of functions. Besides being the most important part of the body from the sexual stimulatory point of view, it represents a vital aspect of our first-line protection against invasion.

The outer layer of the skin is known as the epidermis, and it is covered in most parts of the body by an outer coating of the protein keratin. In areas where there is a great deal of wear and tear, for example the soles of the feet and, in many manual workers, the palms of the hands, the keratin thickens, forming a non-cellular layer of horny substance called callus.

Both keratin, and the integrity of the skin's surface as a whole, help to keep the outer surface of our body watertight. We can thus laze in a warm, soapy bubblebath, or float in the Dead Sea or even dive into a contaminated pool or river, without ill effects. If the skin did not offer this type of protection, then bath-time toiletries, salty water, or life-threatening pathogens could wreak havoc upon our internal environments.

Below the keratin, the epidermal cells are arranged in several layers, the deepest of which constantly divide and multiply. These layers renew the outermost 'dead' cells continuously shed through wear and tear. Immediately below them, is the dermal layer (dermis), in which are found the nerves, sweat glands, sebaceous glands (which produce the greasy substance sebum), blood vessels, lymph vessels and hair shafts. Among all these structures, are woven fibres of both elastin (which helps make the skin stretchy), and the protein collagen, giving the skin strength and toughness.

Sebum affords protection in its own way. It helps to maintain the health of the hair, and it forms an oily film over much of the body, thus helping it to repel liquid with which it comes into contact. In addition, it contains fatty acid compounds which help to combat the activity of certain bacteria. Sweat also has a degree of bacteriostatic activity, as do all body fluids, including blood, urine, tears, digestive juices and vaginal secretions.

The expulsive reflexes

'Foreign body' is a general term for a potentially harmful object or particle that has found its way into one of our body's openings or crevices, or has penetrated the skin. A common example is the small bead or other toy little children push up their noses or into their ears when playing. Others include splinters of wood or metal in or under the skin; dirt, gravel or other solid matter introduced on to a raw surface following an abrasion; a piece of grit on the surface of the eye; or a crumb or droplet of liquid that 'goes down the wrong way' when we swallow.

The body's instinctive response to the presence of foreign material, is to eject it as rapidly as possible. Objects introduced into a nostril are likely to cause irritation, discomfort and sometimes, depending how high up they are pushed, the sneezing reflex.

Smaller particles of dirt and dust are also constantly inhaled in the air we breathe. This is especially true in areas where the degree of atmospheric pollution is high. Hairs in the skin lining the nostrils form an effective trap for a number of these, as well as for bacteria. Those particles that are inhaled into the upper portions of the nasal cavities, and further along the airways into the windpipe (trachea) and bronchial tubes, tend to get caught in the constantly moving stream of mucus produced from the cells lining the region.

The mucus is encouraged to flow upwards and outwards by tiny filamentous projections from the cellular lining, called cilia. The cilia, approximately two thousandths of a millimeter in length, waft the stream of mucus in an upward direction like the oars of a boat upon the surface of a river. When mucus containing trapped material reaches the back of the throat, it can be swallowed, coughed up or spat out.

Cigarette smoke paralyses cilial activity, and this is one reason why smokers are apt to collect large quantities of mucus, debris and bacteria in their lungs. The worsening of the cough that many smokers complain of when they give up smoking is due to the reactivation of the cilia's wafting movement. The paralytic effect of cigarette smoke is an interesting example of how inhaled toxic pollution can weaken the body's natural protective mechanisms.

Coughing can be a voluntary action, or a reflex expulsive response to irritation within the airways or lungs. It helps to get rid of excessive secretions, and, since coughing necessitates the taking of deep breaths, it also aerates whole areas of lung that may fail under usual conditions to expand properly. People suffering from painful chest complaints, or who habitually take very shallow breaths, tend to accumulate secretions within their lungs. This can lead to the stagnation of mucus and the growth of bacteria.

The cough reflex can also be life-saving. A crumb or drop of liquid that reaches the epiglottis (the 'lid' protecting the larynx or voice box), or passes this gateway to the trachea, or windpipe, beyond, causes a violent reaction in a fully conscious person. The coughing and sneezing mechanisms come into play with force, and the victim experiences the intensely frightening sensation of choking. In fact, a serious obstruction that cannot be dislodged in time, can cause death.

More often than not, though, the force of the air expelled from the lungs, can reach velocities of between seventy-five and one hundred miles per hour, well in excess of hurricane force! Most foreign bodies are dislodged in this way.

Noxious gases, and air pollutants which are apparent from their smell or their visible effect upon the air containing them, also evoke a vigorous cough reflex. Escaping household gas, both mains and bottled, fortunately possess a characteristic odour, as do a variety of industrial gaseous wastes. More worrying are the airborne contaminants which remain undetectable to our senses, and yet may well be extremely toxic to our bodies.

A foreign body in the eye causes extreme discomfort. The front of the eye is covered by a sensitive membrane of 'skin', the cornea, which can become easily damaged by a sharp, scratchy piece of grit or sand. Awareness of 'something in the eye' produces an urgent need to remove the irritant immediately. It also activates the tear-producing apparatus situated in the inner corner of the eye and communicating with the interior of the nose.

The copious production of tears aids the body's natural tendency to expel the particle as soon as possible.

The stomach and bowel

The stomach plays an important part in our first-line defence against injurious outside influences. Its most important action in this context, like that of the bowel, is also an expulsive one. However, the stomach deserves separate mention as part of our first-line defence mechanisms as it possesses other means for dealing with foreign material and toxic substances. And from the anatomical point of view, it makes sense to discuss the bowel immediately after the stomach.

Among the injurious outside influences which can make their way to the stomach are foreign bodies inadvertently swallowed together with food or drink, poisonous compounds taken either by accident or with suicidal intent, and pathogens capable of causing damage to the body, either through their own presence or through toxins which they secrete.

Foreign bodies are easier to swallow than one might imagine. Recipe books providing pulse recipes nearly always advice the reader to search for debris among dried lentils and beans. Unwelcome objects can also be encountered in commercially prepared foods and drinks, the wide variety reported in the press ranging from contact lenses, to fragments of tooth and bone, hair pins, rings and pieces of sticking plaster.

While large objects are likely to make their presence felt when they contact the teeth or tongue, tiny pieces of grit and other small items can slide down the food pipe (oesophagus) without drawing attention to themselves. Any damage they cause to the delicate stomach lining, will cause upper abdominal pain and lead, hopefully, to investigation by X-ray. Smaller fragments are dealt with and passed into the small bowel surrounded by a protective layer of partially digested food and mucus, and eventually passed from the bowel without subsequent damage occurring.

Harmful irritants and poisons, on the other hand, are liable to bring the stomach's primary defence mechanism into operation – that of vomiting. When a caustic substance such as strong acid or alkali has been swallowed, the vomiting reflex may cause further damage by the passage of the poison up the food pipe again and into the mouth. In addition, this can injure the wall of the stomach by the churning and expulsive activity characteristic of the action of vomiting.

By and large, though, the ability of the stomach to eject harmful substances shortly after receiving them, represents a very valuable form of protection from harmful external agents. Certain types of food poisoning, for instance that which follows upon the ingestion of food or drink contaminated with Staphylococcal bacteria toxin, frequently produce profuse vomiting within hours of ingestion. Unpleasant though such an attack is, the acute stage of the illness is frequently over within hours, and if ejection of the contaminated substance by vomiting is sufficiently thorough, diarrhoea may well not ensue.

Besides caustic agents and pathogenic organisms, noxious agents taken into the stomach can include chemical contaminants such as lead from old-fashioned water pipes or water vessels, substances accidentally introduced into factory-produced food during manufacture, and poisonous pesticides from unwashed fruit picked from recently sprayed trees.

Others are naturally poisonous plants (eg, poisonous berries, certain toadstools, laburnum seeds), and substances – although wholesome to most people – to which particular individuals are allergic. Typical examples are alcohol, strawberries, mushrooms, commercially prepared icecream, and ham, bacon and pork and any food items containing these.

Another first-line defence mechanism provided by the stomach is that of the acidity of the gastric juice secreted by its lining cells. The stomach wall contains both mucus-secreting cells and others capable of secreting hydrochloric acid and the enzyme pepsin, which helps to digest protein in the food.

The acidity of the gastric juice at rest, that is when the stomach is empty, is around 3 on the pH scale in which 1 represents maximal acidity, 14 maximal alkalinity, and 7, neutrality. (The scale is a logarithmic one, so the difference between two of its units is ten-fold. A resting pH of 3 indicates, therefore, a degree of acidity one hundred times greater than a pH of 5, and ten thousand times greater than neutrality at 7.)

When the stomach is actively stimulated to secrete gastric juice by the arrival of food within it, its pH drops below 3, and can reach 1. A solution of such acidity is able to kill most harmful bacteria and many noxious substances. The highly acid gastric juice does not, under normal conditions, have an adverse effect upon the stomach lining because its cells are protected from injury by a coating barrier of mucus.

Peptic ulcers are inclined to form, either within the stomach or within the first part of the small bowel (duodenum) if the pH of the stomach contents remains at an abnormally low level. Anxiety, nicotine and caffeine all increase the outpouring of excessive gastric acid into the stomach, and its corrosive action is then able to damage the lining. Continuous contact with the highly acidic juice then prevents healing from occurring. Smoking, and drinking large quantities of cola and/or coffee can therefore have a damaging effect upon this important first-line defence mechanism.

The large bowel (or colon) also provides a protective action against serious damage from noxious agents. Toxins, allergens, poisons and other harmful substances may all produce profuse diarrhoea if they do not stimulate vomiting and therefore succeed in reaching the large bowel. When diarrhoeic motions are formed, the bowel lining is irritated, and as a result, contracts more frequently and more forcefully than normal.

This action speeds the rate at which its contents are passed along its length to the rectum where they are ejected. The contractions are also responsible for the severe tummy pains, or colic, that frequently accompany an acute attack of diarrhoea.

Like the stomach, the large bowel has a mucosal lining, and one of its functions is the reabsorption of much of the water present in the food residues it receives. This is why normal motions, or stools, are formed and firm. Diarrhoeic stools are loose or fluid, because the passage of the food residue has been too rapid for much of the water to be absorbed. This in itself adds a further dimension to the defence mechanism afforded by diarrhoea: a high water content dilutes the toxin, thus rendering it less harmful.

Helpful bacteria

A further vital first-line defence mechanism is that of our body flora, that is, the populations of 'helpful' bacteria that colonise the nose, throat, ears and mouth, the colon, the vagina and the lower parts of the urinary system. Such bacteria are purposely called helpful rather than simply 'harmless', because they play a definite part in helping to protect the body against dangerous organisms.

The means by which they do this is thought to be threefold. Potentially injurious bacteria need certain nutrients in order to grow and flourish. Indigent populations of useful bacteria probably require the same nutrients, and use up supplies of it before the advancing pathogens are able to obtain enough for themselves. In this circumstance, either the harmful invaders cease to colonise the area, or do so in very small and non-injurious numbers only.

In addition, some useful bacterial flora secrete an antibiotic-like chemical fatal to enemy organisms. A third possibility is that the conditions established by the friendly flora are conducive to their own continued existence, but unsuitable for the co-existence of noxious bacteria. Such an inhospitable milieu may be created in a number of ways. Pervading pH conditions may be too acid or too alkaline for the would-be settlers. Alternatively, one or several constituents in the useful flora's excreted waste material might be anathema to the invaders' vitality.

The normal flora that inhabit a healthy mouth afford a good example of this type of defence in action. There are between sixteen and twenty different types of useful bacteria that are commonly found in this area without causing disease of any kind. A course of antibiotics very commonly kills these organisms as well as the bacterial infection elsewhere in the body.

This side effect is only too familiar to individuals unlucky enough to have to take antibiotic drugs at frequent intervals. Highly unpleasant bacterial infection can supervene. Alternatively, or in addition, fungal infection may occur, oral thrush being a common one in this circumstance. Vaginal thrush is also a frequent outcome in women after a course of antibiotic drugs.

Prolonged courses of antibiotics, as may be prescribed for patients with conditions such as renal disease, certain heart conditions, chronic bronchitis and emphysema, can also indirectly cause serious disease. Profound destruction of the normal bacterial inhabitants of the large bowel, Lactobacilli, can result in such proliferation of injurious organisms that severe damage is done to the internal mucosal lining . . . resulting in subsequent bouts of blood-stained diarrhoea, sometimes accompanied by abdominal pain.

Intestinal thrush, arising for the reasons just outlined, can also have very serious consequences. It is believed that the causative organisms develop long tendrils or 'mycelia' which come into contact with the blood vessels supplying the bowel wall, and burrow into them. This permits the entry into the bloodstream both of the by-products of the fungus's metabolism and of partially digested food.

The presence of foreign material in the blood can cause a wide range of illnesses, especially allergic symptoms whose underlying cause is difficult to detect. Both mental and emotional conditions can also occur, and it is thought that this fungus may produce the chemical acetaldehyde, which is very toxic and capable of interfering with a number of biochemical process.

Thrush fungal colonies can develop their mycelial form in areas other than the bowel. Unpleasant side effects result wherever this occurs, although it is only within the intestinal tract that partially digested food can also enter the bloodstream.

SECOND-LINE DEFENCE

The body's second-line defence mechanisms comprise the means of protection it calls into play when its first line of defence has been successfully breached by invaders. We are primarily interested in invasion of the body by pathogens (bacteria, viruses and so on), but similar reactions occur when other varieties of foreign material enter the bloodstream.

Inflammation

Inflammation (indicated by the suffix '-itis', eg arthritis) is often considered to be harmful, and evidence of its action anywhere in the body frequently leads the sufferer to seek means of alleviating it. While this reaction is quite understandable, it is wrong to consider the inflammatory process *per se* to be a bad thing.

On the contrary, we would be unable to survive without this vital mechanism that protects us from the havoc-wreaking effects of bacteria, viruses, and noxious substances generally. Not only does it deal with the cause of the injury, but it also represents the initial step of the consequent healing process. Its four cardinal signs, redness, heat, pain and swelling, were described for the first time by the Aulus Cornelius Celsus (first century AD), the author of the earliest known Latin medical treatise.

The easiest way to understand the basic facts about how inflammation works is to picture an area of the body being affected by it. Think of a cat scratching the back of your hand, for instance, or the appearance in the bathroom mirror of the back of your throat when it is sore and infected. Even better, perhaps, visualise a child's tonsils during an attack of tonsillitis. Here you will very likely see evidence of an aspect of this defence mechanism in action, that is, the formation of pus.

The first thing to happen after a cut or scratch or when pathogens multiply in an area such as the tonsils or throat, is the release of a chemical substance, histamine, which causes tiny blood vessels, the capillaries, in the immediate neighbourhood to dilate and leak.

Under normal conditions fluid flows from the capillaries into the surrounding tissue but is drawn back again into the interior of the blood vessels by the 'pull' exerted upon it by the blood protein remaining within. This process is known as osmosis, and is the means by which the vital exchange takes place between the blood inside the blood vessels and the tissue cells it has to supply with oxygen and nutriments.

When fluid leakage occurs at the start of the inflammatory process, however, it tends to remain in the surrounding tissue space, rather than returning as it should. This is due to the fact that, as it leaks out following the release of histamine, it is accompanied by the blood proteins that normally remain within. There is thus insufficient osmotic pressure in the capilliaries in the immediate neighbourhood to draw it back in again.

The reaction so far described, accounts for three of the cardinal signs Celsus first noted. The redness and the heat are due to the dilation of the capillaries, which bring the blood in that area nearer to the surface. The swelling is a natural consequence of fluid accumulating at the site of injury. The swelling, in turn, partly accounts for the fourth element, the pain, by pressure on nearby nerve endings.

Another factor responsible for the pain is irritation of the pain-detecting nerve endings by chemicals released during the inflammatory process, or causing it in the first place. Examples of the latter may be toxins released by invading bacteria, or a chemical such as strong acid or alkali dropped by accident on an area of skin.

The fluid from the capillaries, known as tissue exudate, is useful in that it is mildly antiseptic, and because it dilutes toxic substances. The white blood cells within the fluid are known as phagocytes, from the Greek *phagein*, meaning 'to eat', and *kytos*, meaning 'a vessel' (or in this context, more accurately, a 'cell'), because their action is to 'eat', by engulfing and destroying, harmful bacteria, tissue debris, foreign material, parts of damaged, fragmented cells and so on. They shoot out long blunt finger-like extensions called pseudopodia ('false feet') which surround and engulf the particle concerned. Strong enzymes are then secreted to digest it.

The phagocytes from the capillaries are joined by other phagocytic cells already present in the adjoining tissue space. Many phagocytic cells may be killed in the process of engulfing microbes and noxious particles, but they are a vital aspect of our defence and also prepare the way for healing.

(When a perfectly clean cut or scratch is experienced, no toxic substances or pathogens are present to be engulfed. Nevertheless, the injury inevitably damages the cells concerned, and the phagocytes in this situation engage themselves in destroying the fragmented cellular material.)

The most actively phagocytic of the different types of white blood cells, is the neutrophil, so called because of its appearance when stained and viewed through the microscope. Neutrophils are first on the scene when the cause of the inflammation is foreign material of some type, including bacteria. The blood contains relatively large numbers of neutrophils, about four thousand, five hundred per cubic millimeter, the range being from two and a half thousand to seven thousand

The fluid from the capillaries (the 'inflammatory exudate') then clots. It is able to do so because it contains the same blood proteins, including the clotting factors, as whole blood. The clot prevents the irritant from spreading. In cases where the injury is clean, for instance a surgical incision, or where only a few pathogens managed to get by the first-line defence mechanism, and lost their battle with the phagocytes, the clot is also the initial stage of the healing process.

If the cause of the inflammation persists, pus starts to gather. This consists of the inflammatory exudate, bacteria, fragments of injured cell, and phagocytes both active and dead. It may be thick or watery, possibly stained with red blood cells, and sometimes coloured by pigments produced by the bacteria involved.

Pus has to be drained, when it accumulates, before healing can occur. If the wound is slight this can be done by removing the scab under aseptic conditions and squeezing the inflamed area. Alternatively, when an abscess has formed, the pocket of pus can be lanced under local or general anaesthetic by a doctor, who can then scrape out the cavity of the abscess and apply an antiseptic dressing.

Healing following inflammation may start with the two edges of a clean, narrow cut coming together and healing easily (by what is called 'first intention'). Alternatively, new tissue grows within the clot, initially consisting of new blood vessels and strands of fibrous tissue and later of the characteristic tissue of that area of the body. (This is healing by 'second intention'). Exceptions include muscle and nerve cells, which cannot reproduce themselves, in contrast to skin, bone and capillaries which reproduce themselves very ably.

Inflammation can be either acute or chronic. Examples of the former include a septic spot or boil, colds and sore throats, most types of cystitis (inflammation of the bladder), cholecystitis (inflammation of the gall bladder), and appendicitis. Chronic varieties last longer, produce less dramatic effects, and can cause much lasting damage to the organs affected, by the formation of fibrous scar tissue. Examples of chronic inflammatory illnesses due to infection are syphilis and tuberculosis.

Acute inflammation of a sufficiently severe nature generally produces effects throughout the body. A small, inflamed scratch on the skin of a healthy person will heal without causing generalised symptoms; but even a large, pus-filled whitlow (infection at the side of the finger nail) can cause fever and lassitude, especially if the sufferer is in a run-down condition to start with. Besides a raised body temperature, the pulse rate and sometimes the breathing rate are increased, and antibodies are formed by the immune defence system (see Chapter 4) against the causative bacteria.

Inflammation can also arise as a form of malfunction. In such instances, the immune defence system mistakes harmless substances as potentially threatening, and forms antibodies that produce symptoms of an illness. When the stimulus is a substance in the external environment, such as a particular type of food or drink, cosmetics, clothing or jewellery, the consequent symptoms constitute an 'allergic reaction'. The stimulus is then known as an allergen.

Sometimes, the immune defences of the body are turned against its own tissues, and produce antibodies against them in ways that do a great deal of harm. The underlying condition is known as a state of auto-immunity. Examples of auto-immune illnesses include rheumatoid arthritis, certain types of thyroid disease, ulcerative colitis and pernicious anaemia.

The filtering system

This is another very important aspect of our second-line defence system, and it removes dead cells and foreign or toxic matter from the body. It is known as the reticuloendothelial or RE system (RES) and its cells are found in the lining of blood and 'lymph' (see below) vessels, the lymph nodes, spleen and liver.

The community of cells of which the RE system consists are of several different types, an important one being the 'fixed-tissue macrophage'. This remains in one particular area of the RE system, such as the spleen, and does not migrate. Another is the 'histiocyte' (a 'non-fixed-tissue' macrophage) which can move around, and is an active scavenger, playing an important part in clearing up debris after a skirmish between the RE system and a pathogenic invader.

How the RE cells as a body constitute such an effective defence barrier against the numerous factors capable of upsetting the internal equilibrium, can best be understood by looking briefly at the various parts of the body in which they are to be found.

The lymphatic system consists of lymph vessels or channels with one-way valves, comparable to small, thin veins, distributed throughout the body. These are connected with the groups of lymph nodes (lymph glands) found at various points throughout the body. The tender 'swollen glands' that can be easily felt in the neck as rubbery, rounded nodules are familiar to everyone who has suffered from a throat infection, or nursed a child with measles or tonsillitis. Other areas where groups of lymph nodes exist include the armpits, the groin, the roots of the lungs and around the large veins draining the abdomen and the pelvis. Also part of the lymphatic system is the thymus gland in the upper chest; this consists largely of developing lymphocytes.

The lymph is formed from the tissue fluid that passes under normal conditions from the capillaries into the surrounding tissue space due to the pressure within these small blood vessels (see 'Inflammation' above). Most of it is drawn back into the capillaries by the osmotic effect of the blood proteins that remain within, but additional drainage facilities for tissue fluid exist in the form of the lymphatic system.

The small quantity of protein that *is* present in the tissue fluid, becomes concentrated in the lymphatic fluid. (In all other respects, tissue fluid circulating in and out through the capillary walls, and lymph, have similar compositions.) The lymph also carries away bacteria and other particles too large to pass through the capillary walls. If the lymphatic vessels become blocked, tissue fluid and protein collect in the undrained area. The accumulating protein draws further fluid out through the capillary walls, and a large quantity of tissue fluid gathers. This condition is known as oedema.

Having entered the lymph vessels, the lymph as it then becomes is pumped along by the massaging effect of contracting nearby muscles. Small lymph vessels unite to form larger ones, encountering various groups of lymph nodes *en route* to their final place of termination, the large veins at the root of the neck.

The main channel returning lymph from the upper part of the right side of the body is called the right lymphatic duct, while that draining lymph from the rest of the body is known as the thoracic duct. The lymph nodes, containing resident RE cells supported within a sieve-like framework, filter off debris present either freely in the lymphatic stream as it percolates through them, or contained within phagocytic cells that have already engulfed them. The lymph nodes also manufacture lymphocytes, as well as antibodies when the immune defence system (see next chapter) is brought into play.

The RE cells within the liver and the spleen are arranged throughout these organs within a network of channels, or sinusoids. Thus the internal structure of these organs resembles that of the lymph glands, but blood rather than lymph is percolating through.

These RE cells perform the same task as in the lymph glands, that is, they filter off debris, toxic matter, bacteria, fragmented cells and other particles. Such material is present in the blood, either because it has escaped the filtering process within the lymphatic system proper, or because it has entered the bloodstream directly without first coming into contact with the lymph.

In chapter 4, we will look at the body's most potent weapon against the threat of invasion, the immune defence system itself.

4 Infection and Natural Immunity

We have already dealt with the general protective measures that maintain our equilibrium or homoestasis, despite the challenges of an ever-changing environment and our own frequently changing needs. The immune system however is part of our second line of defence against harmful environmental factors. When working properly it is the most effective and sophisticated means we have of coping with invasion by harmful organisms.

THE HISTORY OF INFECTION

In order to appreciate how important a part the immune defence system plays in keeping us healthy, it is necessary to have some idea of the threat to life and well-being that uncontrolled infectious illnesses can impose. Nowadays, we tend to take freedom from the major infections for granted, chiefly because so many of those that have proved deadly on a massive scale in the past have now been brought under control. Some dreaded scourges, such as smallpox, have been wiped out.

Improved scientific knowledge of pathogenic organisms and their habits has been largely responsible for this progress, and has been the foundation upon which the concept of public health has been built: efficient public and private sanitation; cleaner and better ventilated factories and offices; a bacteria-free public water supply; stringent rules about the commercial preparation, storage and provision of food; and vermin and pest control have all contributed in significant ways to the reduction in deaths due to virulent infections.

Of equal importance has been the development of the science

and art of microbiology, which has led to the identification of an enormous range of bacteria, viruses, parasites and fungi, as well as the development of effective drugs with which to treat the infections they cause.

It took man centuries, however, to realise the true nature of infectious illnesses. A brief description of how the truth dawned gradually throughout centuries of concentrated and inspired effort, makes for a fuller comprehension of the nature of infectious disease, and of how our bodies react to them. As is so often the case in the history of medicine, we return through time to ancient Greece to begin the account.

The philosopher Thucydides provides us with an appropriate starting point. He described a great pestilence that rocked the country in 430BC. Interestingly, he made the first ever recorded reference to immunity, when he said that people were frightened of catching the disease from one another, but that those who caught it and survived, did not catch it again.

The Greek physician Galen, in the second century AD, believed fevers to be due to disorders of the four humours, that is, blood, phlegm, yellow bile and black bile. These were supposed to cause diseases through getting out of balance, and health was thought to be restored by restoring humoral harmony.

Later, in Italy this time, Boccaccio, at the beginning of his *Decameron*, stated that the plague was caught, not only by being in the presence of the sick but also by touching anything they had touched. Generally, however, infectious diseases occurring on a large scale were attributed to unfavourable environmental and climatic conditions. Hippocrates (born around 460BC) favoured this idea, and accurately described in his writings the type of climatic conditions that favour a variety of infectious illnesses.

Certainly, areas where epidemics broke out were shunned by all those aware of the outbreak. The unfortunate inhabitants of affected towns and cities had no other choice than to pile their possessions, children, and small domestic animals into horse-drawn carts and escape pestilence as though it were an invasion by a deadly enemy. Which was, of course, the case.

Even as late as 1854, the general consensus of medical opinion about a cholera outbreak in London was that it was due to noxious vapours in the atmosphere (see 'Doctors and Infection' below).

A sixteenth-century manuscript provides us with the first general account of infection. Fracastorius of Verona (1546) described 'seeds of contagion' that could pass on infectious illnesses through direct contact with the patient, through touching objects a patient had handled, or even at a distance. A German priest, Athanasius Kircher, around 1650, was the first to suggest that germs, or Fracastorius's 'seeds of contagion' might be small living things. The famous Dutch microbiologist and microscopist, Anton van Leeuwenhoek (1632–1723), published his findings in 1683, describing and drawing the various types of microbes (single-celled animals, or protozoa, and bacteria), he had been able to see with his microsope. But the essential connection between these living creatures and infectious illnesses was not made until a century and a half later.

Controversy raged throughout this period over whether the microbes caused the disease, or the disease, the microbes. This confusion may seem very strange to us now, but one has to remember that scientists had precious little evidence at their disposal. All they knew for certain was that infectious illness spread quickly from one person to another and that in specimens of saliva, phlegm, blood, urine, faeces, and so on small living objects appeared to exist.

Putrefaction and infection were not connected, however. Many renowned scientists were, in fact, firmly convinced of spontaneous generation, that is, the ability of decaying matter to generate new life. Maggots appearing in stale meat, for instance, were thought to be evidence of this. 'Proof' was produced, first for one side of the argument and then for the other, with supporters of each theory ignoring and ridiculing the findings and deductions made by their opponents.

In this instance, as in so many in the history of scientific thought, pursuers of the truth became so engrossed in 'winning' the fight and proving themselves right, that they abandoned their vital faculty of objective and unprejudiced judgment.

The French chemist Louis Pasteur (1822–95) finally solved the problem. He was able to prove conclusively that the souring of milk, and the fermentation of alcoholic beverages was due to living microbes (bacteria and yeast respectively), and then that putrefaction and infection were due to a similar cause.

The German scientist, Robert Koch (1843–1910), a contemporary of Pasteur, then established for all time that microbes are the cause of infectious illnesses. He also showed how any particular infection can be ascribed to its causative microbe and no other, despite the fact that specimens taken from infected patients invariably contain both the causative organism and others which are in no way responsible. In doing so, he laid down the fundamental principles of clinical bacteriology, of which science he is regarded as the founder.

The existence of viruses was discovered initially by deductive reasoning from circumstantial evidence, for their presence could not be detected by the microscope on account of their minute size. They could not be demonstrated as colonies of growth by Koch's bacterial culture methods, either, since viruses need living tissue cells in which to grow and multiply. Foot and mouth disease of cattle was one of the first diseases to be attributed to viral infection (1898).

By 1931, a method had been designed for culturing pure strains of viruses within chick embryos, one of the methods still used today. And in 1938, it was possible for the first time to photograph a virus, by means of the electron microscope.

The meaning of infection

For true infection to be present, pathogens have to thrive and multiply, and cause some ill effect in their host. As we saw in the previous chapter, the mere presence of bacteria, or for that matter viruses, on an area of skin or within an area such as the anal canal or the cavity of the mouth, does not constitute an infection. An infection causes real problems to the host, and produces symptoms that need to be dealt with.

True infection invariably follows a 'silent' period of incubation. This is the interval of time between the pathogens successfully overcoming our defence barriers and setting up thriving colonies, and the appearance of symptoms. This time lapse may be as short as an hour in some forms of extremely severe food poisoning, and may take months, or even years, in the case of a disease such as AIDS (acquired immuno deficiency syndrome), but tends to be constant for any given disease.

Bacterial infections generally reveal signs of themselves sooner than viral infections. This is because, when viruses enter the body, time passes before they reach their 'target' organ and get down to the business of division and multiplication within the tissue cells. Colds and influenza are exceptions to this rule, because they can start right away in the tissue cells of the respiratory tract which they invade in the first place. Bacteria, by way of contrast to the majority of viruses, can 'get going' right away.

Once the incubation period is over, inflammation in the colonised area begins to appear, generally coupled with the toxic effects of poisons which the pathogens put out. Bacterial toxins are of two varieties. Endotoxins ('inside poisons') are within the bacteria themselves, and are released into the tissues when the bacteria are killed by defence mechanisms. Exotoxins ('outside poisons') are secreted by intact bacteria and get carried away by the bloodsteam, producing effects elsewhere in the body. Tetanus bacteria release a toxin which travels from the skin wound where they enter the body and affects the nervous system.

The growth of awareness

Prior to Pasteur's work, infectious illnesses were almost impossible to treat effectively. Quinine was found to be effective against malaria in the seventeenth century, and mercury against syphilis in the sixteenth century. Herbal remedies were commonly used, some with excellent effect and others with little benefit to the patient. Samuel Hahnemann introduced homoeopathy as a system of medicine at the beginning of the nineteenth century, and it was found to be more effective than orthodox treatment during the great cholera epidemics of that century.

In fact, in 1854, when the figures were collected for the mortality rates in London hospitals, the record for the homoeopathic hospital was so superior to all the others that at first the Board of Health, dominated by orthodox doctors, tried to suppress the figures by leaving them out of the published record! They were only prevented from doing so by the intervention of a young politician, whose sympathies lay with homoeopathic treatment.

Injury wounds almost invariably became infected, and surgical procedures were as hazardous from the point of view of post-operative infection as they were from the trauma inflicted by the relatively crude surgical methods of the time.

Death from puerperal fever (infection following childbirth) was also extremely common until the mid-nineteenth century. As delivery in hospital became the rule rather than the exception, infection became rife as it spread from one patient to another. Paradoxically, physical contact with nurses and doctors unaware of carrying the infectious organisms on their hands and on apparatus and instruments, was a prime cause of the spread. In some hospitals, the death rate among nursing mothers was as high as twenty-five per cent.

In 1861, however, the famous Hungarian obstetrician Ignaz Semmelweis (1818–65) published an account of his research into the cause of puerperal fever, and became a major pioneer in its prevention. He noted that a friend who died of blood-poisoning after carrying out a post-mortem, had before he died developed the same symptoms as the women. Although the role of pathogens had not yet been established, he had observed earlier that the death toll from the disease was considerably higher in the wards where medical students were taught than it was in those where student midwives were taught. He observed that the medical students went straight from the post-mortem room to the labour ward to deliver babies, and he concluded that they in some way carried the infection with them. Thereafter, he insisted that everyone attending a confinement should first wash their hands in chlorine water, a strong antiseptic. The death rate fell by ninety per cent as a result. It is one of the great ironies in the history of medicine, however, that Semmelweis's revelations caused him so much abuse and hostility from his colleagues in Vienna where he was currently practising, that he had to leave Austria and return to his native Hungary.

There are many other physicians and surgeons who contributed to progress in the fight against infectious diseases. Edward Jenner (1749–1843) introduced vaccination (see below) against smallpox as early as 1796. John Snow (1813–58), a London doctor and the first specialist in anaesthesia, put a stop to a cholera outbreak by tracing its source to an infected water supply. Lord Joseph Lister (1827–1912), the famous professor of surgery in Glasgow, Edinburgh and London sequentially, published a paper on antiseptic surgery in 1867, and made the treatment of surgical and other wounds incalculably safer through his use of carbolic acid dressings and spray. While safe surgery was developing apace, Pasteur and other bacteriologists were developing the science of vaccination beyond its established use in the prevention of smallpox.

Antibiotic drugs

During the present century, potent drugs against pathogenic infection have been discovered. In 1911, the German scientist Paul Ehrlich (1854–1915) (well known to biology students the world over for his bacteriological stain known as Ehrlich's haemotoxylin) introduced salvarsan for the treatment of syphilis. This was the first drug ever to be manufactured as specific treatment for the cause of an illness.

Salvarsan, modified four years later to the safer compound neosalvarsan, became the prototype upon which many antibacterial drugs have since been modelled. Paul Ehrlich also won a Nobel prize for his research into the immune reaction, and is one of the pioneers of modern immunological science.

Two further names must be mentioned in this context, both contributors of immensely important drugs in the field of anti-bacterial therapy. Firstly, Gerhard Domagk (1895–1964), a German pathologist and Nobel prize winner, whose research led to the discovery of further drugs that could treat bacterial diseases yet remain safe for the patient to take. He is especially renowned for his production of protonsil, the first sulphonamide, active against Streptococcal bacteria, and for isoniazid, effective against tuberculosis.

Secondly, Sir Alexander Fleming (1881–1955), bacteriologist and surgeon at St Mary's hospital, London, discovered the effectiveness of penicillin mould against Staphylococcal bacteria in 1928. This finding sadly made little impression on Fleming's colleagues, until Florey and Chain, two brilliant chemists with whom Fleming shared a Nobel prize for medicine in 1945, perfected a method eleven years later of producing this volatile drug.

Since 1950, effective anti-tuberculous drugs including Domagk's isoniazid have been in general use, and few people die of tuberculosis nowadays. In addition to effective drug therapy, research continues into the complexities of the immune response, aimed at the development of more effective methods of preventing infections by immunisation.

WHAT IMMUNITY MEANS

Immunity simply means 'not liable to danger from'. Immunity to a particular infection implies that we can encounter the organism responsible for it with safety, since we are protected against its potential ill effects. The secret of this protection is the essence of immune defence function, that is, the ability to distinguish between 'self' and 'non-self'. The practical outcome of this ability is the formation of the protein molecule called the 'antibody'.

Considering the millions of different bacteria, viruses, fungi and single-celled parasites that exist, there are relatively few that constitute a direct threat to our well-being. Our habitual environment, wherever that may be, by definition can contain only a limited number of pathogenic types. Although practically nothing is unheard of in clinical medicine, you would be excessively unlikely to contract malaria at a Wembley stadium football match in London, leprosy while on holiday in the south of France, or Rocky Mountain Spotted Fever while climbing the Pennines in the north of England.

On the other hand, you may well catch a typical head cold while on holiday at the Equator, tuberculosis in the UK if you had sufficient contact with an 'active' carrier, or typhoid anywhere in the world from a contaminated water supply. This illustrates as simply as possible that certain conditions, such as the Western climate, preclude almost entirely the successful survival of many pathogens and their intermediate hosts. An example is the Anopheline mosquito carrying the single-celled Plasmodium parasite responsible for outbreaks of malaria.

On the other hand, certain types of bacteria and viruses are more or less ubiquitous, those responsible for the common cold and influenza among them, despite the fact that the strains (varieties) of the causative organisms differ from location to location.

Apart from the natural restrictions on exposure afforded by geographical location and climate, our bodies provide a suitable environment for a limited number only of the thousands of species that might stage a successful invasion. It is very unusual indeed, for example, to suffer from blood poisoning (septicaemia) as a result of a surgical operation on the cavity of the mouth (buccal cavity) or on the nasal passages and sinuses. Bacteria normally resident in these areas unavoidably get into the bloodstream when an incision is made, and can be detected in samples of blood taken for a short time afterwards. Nevertheless, no ill effects are encountered except in rare circumstances, because the bacteria concerned cannot multiply and establish themselves within the human system. This type of protection results quite simply from the would-be parasites' requirements differing from those afforded by their host. It is not an application of the immune reaction.

A corollary of this is the fact that, like other parasites, many bacteria and viruses are restricted by reason of their specific metabolic needs, to infesting only one or two types of host. The organism *Chlamydia psittaci*, for instance, which causes psittacosis (ornithosis, parrot fever), is transmitted to man by a variety of birds. Discovered for the first time in a parrot (hence the name, which is derived from the Greek word for parrot), psittacosis is now known to infect several different species of bird, including domestic fowl (chickens, ducks, turkeys), budgerigars, pigeons, parakeets and pheasants.

Man and birds, however, are the only hosts in which the organism can survive. The infection is commonest among habitual bird handlers, and is most often transmitted from bird to man through the inhalation of dried, infected excrement. Eating the flesh of infected fowl cannot transmit the infection. This calls into play the protection against invasion provided by the gastric juices of the stomach, which *Chlamydia psittaci* is unable to withstand.

In contrast to psittacosis, avian TB (tuberculosis in birds) cannot be transmitted to man. Hence, man and other animals are often safe in contact with bacteria which can cause grave illness and death in another species.

THE IMMUNE REACTION

In identifying invading pathogens as 'non-self' and harmful, the antibodies which the immune defence system thereupon manufactures are deadly to the unwanted invader in a very special way. Their function is to render the pathogen harmless, and the explanation for the excellence with which they are fitted to this task, is their absolute specificity to the pathogen (ie, the antigen) which they encounter.

This is significant in two ways. Firstly, the antibody evoked by a particular pathogen is uniquely suited to incapacitate it. Secondly, the ability to produce that specific antibody is retained by the immune system, so that further encounters with the same strain of pathogen will evoke the same protective response.

Humoral immunity

This is the sequence of events the acute immune reaction (also known as humoral immunity) is believed to follow. When a pathogen meets the body's first- and second-line defences, it is detected as 'non-self', or antigenic, by the body. It comes into contact with a macrophage which engulfs it and breaks it up into small units.

The macrophage then meets a lymphocyte and passes on information about the nature of the antigen it has ingested. In this way, the immune system obtains an exact description of the configuration of the required antibody. The lymphocyte transforms itself into a plasma cell, and starts to manufacture antibodies accordingly. This particular variety of lymphocyte is known as a B cell or B lymphocyte, to differentiate it from the T cell or T lymphocyte involved in the second variety of immune response, the delayed hypersensitivity reaction (see 'Cellular immunity' below).

The specificity of the antibody in any given instance is dictated by particular groupings of molecules within the structure of the bacteria or virus with which it is designed to deal. These spatially arranged molecular groupings are the specific antigenic sites which enable the body to recognise the pathogen as 'foreign' when invasion first occurs. The sites are peculiar to each strain of bacterium or virus, which means that antibodies against, for example, a specific strain of Streptococcal bacteria (responsible for bad sore throats) will always be capable of dealing with that particular strain, and only that particular strain, should it invade again.

Another strain of Streptococcus, however similar to the first, would have slightly different antigenic characteristics. A new set of antibodies would accordingly have to be synthesised to deal with these.

The protein molecules of which the antibodies consist, are modelled in such a way that their shape enables them to fit precisely into the corresponding antigenic site on the surface of the pathogen. An exact analogy is the way with which the 'right' key fits a lock, or the 'right' piece of a jigsaw puzzle precisely fits the space it is designed to fill. Most antibodies have two active sites which fit that of an antigenic configuration. This means that one antibody can incapacitate and link up two antigens.

All living protein, including human tissue cells, is provided with a set of identification marks or 'immune markers' (antigenic sites) such as these. This is why our bodies react against foreign tissue when they encounter it in the form of an organ transplant, a skin graft or sometimes a blood transfusion. Antibody formation, undesirable in such circumstances, is the explanation for the rejection problems transplantation surgery is endeavouring to overcome.

Antibodies are produced in this way in the lymph nodes and other lymphatic tissue. They are then released into the bloodstream, where they are referred to as 'humoral antibodies', because the blood was one of the 'humours' of the body in earlier medical history. They travel around the body, where their primary aim is to attack and destroy the bacteria against which they have been formed.

They do this by attaching themselves to the cell wall of the bacteria, one antibody sometimes linking two antigens by virtue of its dual receptor sites. In this way, small clumps of captured bacteria can be formed, and these are easier for the RE system to catch than single bacteria. A further useful feature of the humoral immunity reaction is the existence of a group of substances known as the 'complement' system. These help the antibodies to break up and destroy the bacteria, the debris of which are then engulfed and digested by phagocytes.

The production of antibodies to an antigenic stimulus not previously encountered takes place over about seven to ten days; this is generally the earliest at which the antibodies can be detected in a sample of patient's blood. The re-production of antibodies previously formed, however, occurs much more rapidly, sometimes within hours of the second or subsequent meeting with the antigen.

This remains the case even when many years separate the two events. Thus contact with an active measles virus will generally produce the symptoms of the illness in a child or adult who has not acquired earlier immunity. While the illness is developing and progressing, however, antibodies against the measles virus are being synthesised. Subsequent exposure to this same viral strain will not – except in very unusual circumstances – result in a second attack, immunity having been acquired.

Antibody synthesis

There are several possible explanations for the formation of antibodies. The theory propounded above, that the arrival of the antigen within the body in some way stimulates the formation of a suitable antidote to itself, is one of the most usual and useful. This is known as the 'template' theory, and assumes that a 'mould' is made of the determining antigenic site, and that from this mould an appropriately shaped antibody can then be synthesised.

The 'selective' theory, on the other hand, suggests that we contain within us at birth, templates of all the antibodies we could ever be expected to require, within individual cells. An encounter with an antigen 'selects' the appropriate antibody-forming cell and stimulates it to multiply rapidly, producing numerous other identical cells (called collectively 'clones'), all possessing the ability to manufacture the specific antibody required.

Cellular immunity

The formation of humoral antibodies is the immediate response of the immune defence system to sudden invasion by most pathogenic bacteria and viruses. The second type of immune reaction, however, is designed to deal with a number of other pathogens upon which humoral antibodies would have little effect.

They are organisms which are capable of living and growing within the cells that engulf them, and they include certain viruses, bacteria such as the tuberculosis and leprosy bacilli, fungi and protozoal parasites. This second variety of response is believed to work as follows.

The organism spends the early part of its time in the body outside the cells it is later to penetrate. During this brief interval, its presence in the blood and tissues evokes the synthesis of specifically sensitised lymphocytes known as T cells or T cell lymphocytes. Once the pathogen has invaded the cells it intends to inhabit, these lymphocytes identify the cells concerned and release a number of chemical substances. These, in addition to other stimuli, cause the number of macrophages in the area to rise dramatically, enlarge in size, and increase in potency.

This means that that their ability to secrete enzymes is increased, and that their output of other products also rises. The result of this macrophage activation is that they develop more potent micro-biocidal and cytotoxic activity, that is, they are more readily able to kill both pathogenic organisms and the cells in which the invading pathogens have taken up residence.

Macrophage activation takes place gradually over hours or days, in contrast to the metabolic burst of activity that typifies phagocytosis which occurs over a matter of seconds or minutes. (A similar acceleration of chemical activity is seen when macrophages are suddenly subjected to certain stimuli in their immediate environ-ment.) During the course of this 'delayed hypersensitivity' response even the sensitised T cells join the battle, and kill some of the pathogen-ridden cells themselves.

T cells also release other chemical mediators, the best known of which is 'transfer factor'. This substance appears capable of transferring delayed hypersensitivity to specific antigens, from the sensitised T cells that produce it, to other neighbouring non-sensitised lymphocytes that have met the antigen in question. This factor may be released from the T cells as rapidly as one hour after their contact with the antigen. Once the unsensitised lymphocytes receive the transfer factor, they are then able to begin synthesising the required antibody themselves, and also dividing and multi-plying. In this way, availability of aggressive lymphocytes capable of handling the enemy pathogen is enormously increased, and the enemy pathogen itself becomes part of the process.

T cells are also thought to be capable of transferring this immunological boost from one human subject to another requiring it. One instance in which this reaction has been studied has involved the transference of delayed sensitivity (ie, cellular immunity) to tuberculin (a protein derived from the tuberculosis bacilli, and used for testing immunity to this illness). Another has involved transferring cellular immunity in a similar way, to diphtheria toxoid, the treated toxin of the diphtheria bacterium used in immunisation against this infection.

Transfer factor has aroused considerable interest because of its potential therapeutic value. Patients with certain fungal infections, immune deficiency disorders, and even some cancer patients have received injections of concentrated material prepared from donor lymphocytes. The aim has been the transference of a cellular immunity that may come to the aid of these patients' own immune response. There is some evidence that this method of treatment may prove of value in the future.

When a pathogen evokes the cellular immune reaction for the first time, the invading viruses and the sensitised T lymphocytes may be seen as engaged in a race against time. The object of the former is to colonise the host as effectively as possible, and the object of the latter is to thwart this aim at every turn.

Should the same variety of pathogenic organism invade on subsequent occasions, the chances are weighted heavily in favour of the success of the sensitised T lymphocytes, a sizeable colony of which is already present against further attacks. These are capable of multiplying their own number and producing antibodies at a sufficiently swift rate to overpower the multiplying virus. This is the concept upon which the practice of immunisation is founded although, for safety's sake, dead or modified forms of the pathogens are used to provoke the required response in preference to the live, virulent forms.

Besides transfer factor, lymphocytes produce a number of other chemical mediators playing important roles in the immune response. One of these is called 'interferon', and has been found to possess both antiviral and antitumour properties. Its mode of action is as yet unclear, although it is known to stimulate the antitumour activity of natural killer cells (ie lymphocytes which have nonspecific actions lethal to tumour tissue). A type of interferon is produced commercially from human tissue cell cultures, and used with varying amounts of success in the treatment of certain types of cancer.

Immunisation

There are two main types of immunity. The first is the less important of the two and is known as 'passive immunity'. This refers to the conferring of immunity to a person suffering from an infectious illness or at special risk of catching it, by the injection of antibodies known as antitoxins. Tetanus antitoxin was the first to be isolated, in Robert Koch's laboratory in 1890, two years after the isolation under Pasteur's direction of the specific toxin responsible for the symptoms of diphtheria.

Protection against both of these diseases is still conferred by means of injected antitoxin, but the effect is relatively brief for there is no stimulus in this procedure to cause the recipient's own immune defence system to manufacture its own antibodies thereafter.

The second type, 'active immunity', refers to the formation of antibodies along the lines discussed above in the section 'What Immunity Means'. This type can come about in two different ways. Firstly, it can result naturally from personal experience of the illness, and secondly, it can be brought about by artificial means, through deliberate immunisation or vaccination.

Edward Jenner (see above), who invented vaccination (a term derived from the Latin *vacca*, a cow), inoculated patients with cowpox virus in order to create in them the desired immunity to the far more deadly illness of smallpox. Inoculation against smallpox had been used in this country for fifty years before vaccination was first introduced, and had consisted of inoculating people deliberately with mild cases of smallpox, in order to allow a mild attack to protect them from then onwards against a really virulent attack.

Jenner's method was effective and a great deal safer, for cow-pox was a relatively benign disease compared with smallpox. The latter claimed many lives during the process of deliberate inoculation, even with very mild cases. Much research has been carried out this century into methods that both attenuate the bacteria sufficiently to render them safe, yet keep them sufficiently virulent to evoke the required immune response.

Pasteur brought the rabies virus to the desired degree of weakened virulence by inoculating one rabbit after another with the organisms. He used this method because, during its passage through successive animals, the virus lost a degree of its potency. By the time the twenty-fifth rabbit had been inoculated, the virus, reclaimed from the rabbit and dried, was safe to use for human vaccination.

The majority of vaccines prepared nowadays, however, are prepared from dead pathogens, as this makes for a safer, if shorter-lasting, preventive measure.

Having looked at the immeasurable benefits of antibiotics to mankind, and also at their possible misuse, the harm they can in some circumstances cause, and how the strength of the immune defence system can be impaired by many everyday factors, we are going to look at ways of strengthening our own natural defences.

5 Self Help through Fasting and Food

A great deal of nonsense is written (and talked) about fasting. It has developed a reputation as a cranky practice advocated by alternative practitioners for the cure of every ill under the sun. Its followers are popularly supposed to be odd-looking individuals who frequent health food stores for the occasional packet of dried seaweed or tofu pâté between periods of self-imposed starvation.

The quasi-religious concept of fasting does nothing to improve its image. 'Fasting and prayer' fit naturally into a story book picture of hermit saints in sackcloth and ashes, punishing their bodies for the betterment of their souls. The impressive 'odour of sanctity' emanating from those in an advanced state of spiritual enlightenment was, in fact, the presence of ketones in the breath as a result of abstention from food.

'Fasting' also has a bad name because people associate it with eating disorders such as anorexia nervosa and bulimia, and with the type of crash diet aimed at removing excess weight at a rate of about a pound a day. Many really overweight 'would-be' dieters are terrified of the word. To them, giving up their usual daily mounds of chocolate bars, french fries or crêpes Suzette *feels* exactly like not eating at all. The idea of *actually* doing without food *entirely* for a period of time, is too appalling to contemplate.

The truth is that fasting can be very beneficial. As with so many forms of radical treatment, especially the self-administered variety, it all depends upon how it is done. It is not the same thing as starvation. Starvation is a harmful experience, whether it be self-imposed, or imposed upon an individual for destructive purposes. Far from having a therapeutic effect, it ultimately causes severe metabolic injury and loss of muscle mass, and leads to death if not arrested and reversed in time.

Fasting is carried out with a restorative or curative end in view, and self-administered fasts usually continue for the relatively brief period of one to four days at a time. Fasts of longer duration should be carried out only under expert health guidance and management. Food is carefully reintroduced at the end of the fast, and certain liquids permitted throughout the fasting days.

A further distinction between fasting and starvation, is that no real hunger – apart from the occasional pang during the first few hours – is experienced when a fast is being undergone. Hunger is nearly always severe, however, at least to start off, when starvation is being inflicted.

A fast can be relative or absolute. This is how Roger Newman Turner, the naturopathic specialist, defines the term:

> Fasting is voluntary abstention from food for a given period, which can range from twelve hours to ninety days or more. Most therapeutic fasts are undertaken for three to seven days. Liquid is taken as boiled, or mineral water, or some fruit or vegetable juices.

He then goes on to discuss[4] the therapeutic benefits of this form of treatment, and supplies several examples of modified fasting regimens that permit a little solid food to be taken. The Guelpa, or Saline, fast, for instance, introduces a bowl of thick vegetable soup together with two thin slices of dry wholemeal toast in the evening of the second day, and dry toast or biscuits, perhaps accompanied by a baked potato, on the third day.

HOW FASTING WORKS

The purpose of fasting is to release the accumulated toxins stored in the tissues (see last Chapter 2) and to eliminate them by means of the body's excretory mechanisms. The naturopathic explanation for its frequently beneficial effects is that it mobilises the detoxifying

4. Newman Turner, R. *Naturopathic Medicine* Thorsons Publishers, Wellingborough, UK, page 90

defence mechanisms (particularly the RE system), and stimulates subsequent recuperation. An added bonus is the rest it gives to the digestive system.

An alternative explanation is that it removes allergenic food substances which may normally feature in a person's diet, and provoke symptoms whose underlying cause is frequently very difficult to identify. Fasting is used for this purpose prior to testing for food allergies by both orthodox and alternative medical practitioners.

Here is what Leslie Kenton, has to say in her best-selling *Raw Energy* (Century Publishing Company Ltd, 1984) about the fruit fast. Ms Kenton advocates this for the second and third days of her 'Ten Day Prove-It-To-Yourself Raw Energy Diet'.

> The fruit fast is one of the best ways of clearing your system quickly . . . [it] is effective in several ways. In a purely physical sense fruit is mildly laxative and a wonderful intestinal 'broom' to sweep your alimentary canal clean. Fruit is alkaline-forming; most stored wastes which are responsible for aches and disease in general are acidic. When your body is given the chance to throw off these wastes, as it is on the Prove-It-To-Yourself diet, they first enter the bloodstream. The alkalinity of the fruit helps to neutralise them so that they are not harmful and can be quickly expelled. It this way you minimise the possibility of any cleansing reactions and rapidly achieve a better acid/alkaline balance. Fruit also has a high potassium content. This is helpful in ridding the system and the tissues of excess water, and increasing oxygenation in the cells . . .

Fasting is especially useful in the treatment of feverish infections, such as influenza, tonsillitis, bronchitis and most childhood infections. It can also help other acute conditions such as gastroenteritis and chronic states such as cholecystitis (gall bladder inflammation, sometimes inefective by nature), and asthma, sinusitis and colitis, all of which can possess an infective element.

A further bonus of regular (even if brief) fasting periods is loss of excessive body fat. Besides the obvious attractions of this, we will see below how a healthily low body weight can boost the immune defence system. Weight reduction is not the usual aim of therapeutic fasts, but some overweight people use brief fasting periods in this way because they find that the 'all or nothing' approach suits them better than months of rigid self-denial. This is usually the case when the amount of weight to be lost is either within the range of seven to ten pounds only, or when a great deal of weight requires to be lost and the dieter needs the psychological boost of seeing a few pounds melt away rapidly.

Some people keep slim and fit by fasting for a day or two every week and eating as sensibly as they can – allowing themselves the occasional indulgence – for the rest of the time. It is said that Napoleon was an advocate of this method. Known to be a keen gourmet he ate to his heart's content for six days a week. On the seventh day, he would go out riding for an entire day, in order to remove himself from the tempting sights and smells of the delicacies he loved.

During his day on horseback, he permitted himself only water to drink, and the occasional almond to chew. It must have worked for him, as none of the portraits one sees of him ever make him out to be obese.

Fasting also has the effect that is popularly known as 'shrinking the stomach'. No real reduction in gastric size actually occurs, of course, but one's digestive system gets accustomed to having to deal with comparatively very small quantities, with the result that a little food is more readily satisfying. It also permits the appestat mechanism in the hypothalmic area of the brain, to re-establish control. This means that instead of continuing to stuff food mindlessly until one's 'normal' excessive quantity has been de-molished, one becomes aware of the sensation of being full when one's metabolic needs have been satisfied, which is far sooner than we usually think.

Regarding the benefits to the immune system, fasting as part of a sensible weight reduction programme allows it to function more efficiently. Being fat hampers the activities of the immune defence forces, thus increasing the risk of succumbing to infections. It is important to remember, though, that fasting for a day or so (or even a week) will do nothing for anyone if it is followed by a resumption of usual bad eating habits.

THE BENEFITS OF A LOW-CALORIE DIET

There is further evidence of the benefits to the immune defence system which can be gained from calorie restriction. Two other major functions of this system besides defence against infection, are life extension coupled with the retention of youthfulness, and protection against cancer. Recent research carried out by Roy Walford, Professor of Pathology at the University of Los Angeles Medical School, and his colleagues, has shown that low calorie diets have a profound effect upon laboratory animals, both in extending their (healthy) lifespan, and in reducing their risks of developing malignant disease.

The researchers found that their underfed mice lived far longer than their overfed 'control' mice. Some of the former group, in fact, had their lifespan extended by up to sixty per cent. With reference to this result, Professor Walford commented that he and his colleagues had succeeded in retarding the ageing process in a way that was equivalent in human terms to increasing maximum lifespan from the present length of 110 years to between 150 and 180 years. He also pointed out that this study of laboratory animals is, with a high level of probability, directly translatable to human use.

The Professor stressed that the key concept here is 'undernutrition without malnutrition'. The underfed mice not only lived far longer but also suffered far less than the overfed ones from heart disease and cancer. In an *undernutrition* regimen, the total number of calories is sharply limited but the diet provides all the critical nutrients such as vitamins, minerals, essential amino acids and essential fatty acids.

The low-calorie diet mice also remained sleek and healthy-looking, far longer than others. In human terms, this would mean that they continued looking – and presumably feeling – far younger for far longer than they would have otherwise.

The Walford experiments were not the first to be carried out into the effects of undernutrition on the living organism. The Venetian Luigi Cornaro, who wrote *The Art Of Living Long*, was born in 1464 and lived to be 103 years old. A member of the Italian nobility, his lifestyle was an extreme example of gluttonous self-indulgence until the age of 37, when his health began to suffer. He then cut down his food intake rigorously and ceased to drink alcohol.

He discovered that he enjoyed life a very great deal more once he had started to follow a restricted regimen, since he had more energy, a clearer head, and a great deal more vitality and enthusiasm. It must be remembered that nothing was known at that time in the scientific sense either about our metabolic energy requirements or which foods contained the vital nutrients our bodies need. Cornaro's improved health and longevity can be seen as outstanding examples of the value of following the body's innate curative instincts.

The effects of intermittent fasting on laboratory rats were researched in the 1940s by Professors A. H. Carlson and F. Holzel.

The animals were fed a highly nutritious diet, of which they could eat as much as they pleased. Three separate groups were fasted totally, every second, third and fourth day respectively, and their health and lifespans compared with a 'control' unfasted group fed same diet. The maximum lifespan for the unfasted group was 800 days, and between 1,000 and 1,100 days for all three intermittently fasted groups. This amounted to a twenty to thirty per cent extension of their maximum lifespan.

Professor Walford's experiments differ from the others described here in that he used adult mice with an age equivalent to thirty to thirty-five years in human beings. The rest used weanling animals. Intermittent fasting combined with a highly nutritious diet does not retard growth and development although it prolongs lifespan. The regimen Professor Walford personally follows and recommends is total abstinence from food on two successive days a week, with a healthy, supplemented diet on the other five days. You'll find practical advice about how to go about this yourself later on in this chapter.

In addition to increasing the chances of healthy longevity, other benefits of undernutrition have been listed by the Professor. These include reduced susceptibility to disease, which occurs, if at all, far later in life than is usual; and improved mental and intellectual capabilities. The retention of a considerable degree of physiological and biochemical youthfulness (for example, a lower blood cholesterol level, fewer signs of degeneration in the collagen constituent of connective tissue, a 'younger' rate of metabolism) is a further bonus.

With fewer degenerative changes occurring in 'middle aged' and 'older' laboratory animals, the reduced incidence of cancer in calorie-restricted animals was especially noteworthy. Of the animals who were permitted to indulge to their hearts' content, sixty-five per cent developed cancer, in contrast to only fifteen per cent of those whose food intake was curtailed.

In revealing the beneficial effects of calorie restriction combined with a high nutrition level, Professor Walford and his colleagues emphasised the obvious effects upon the functional ability of the immune defence system. The main indications of this, were the greatly reduced incidence of malignant diseases and degenerative age-related changes, and the increased resistance to diseases of all kinds, including infections.

With advanced age, the ability of the immune defences to protect us from invasion by pathogens and toxic material, declines to between ten and twenty per cent of its peak value in youth. Concurrently, its ability to distinguish between self as 'friend to be protected' and 'non-self to be destroyed' is greatly impaired, with the result that auto-immune and self-destructive processes start to show themselves. This is all part of the usual ageing process, and includes the increased facility with which cancer cells develop into tumours and destructive growths rather than being removed by the immune defences as soon as they appear. Professor Walford says on this topic:

> [Dietary] restriction from time of weaning greatly slows the age-related decline in response to foreign materials. *Restriction beginning in adulthood actually leads to substantial rejuvenation of the immune system.* At the same time, the signs of anti-self reactions are markedly reduced. In humans, part of senile dementia may be caused by antibrain auto-antibodies which occur with ageing. These are greatly reduced by dietary restriction (my italics).

Regarding the effect upon brain development, the Walford experiments have shown that although calorie restriction during the weaning period can greatly reduce the rate of general growth, the brain weights increase at the same rate as in the fully fed animals. That is, brain weight is preserved irrespective of body weight.

A link exists, however, between low body fat and infertility in females. For this reason, Professor Walford suggests that a break from this programme should be taken by women wanting to conceive, and by pregnant women and nursing mothers. In addition, the restriction of calories should be gradually introduced over a five- to seven-year period. The amount of weight that would normally be lost in a non-obese person, would be in the region of a fifth to a quarter of the total body weight.

To provide an example: 1.7m (5ft 8in) man weighing 67kg (10 stone 8lb), might have to lose up to 10 to 15kg (20 to 30lb) to achieve maximum life extension. He would undertake gradual restriction of total calories to about sixty per cent of his unrestricted intake, for instance, from 2,500 calories a day to about 1,600 calories. It seems that the internationally recommended daily calorie allowances of 3,000 for a man, and 2,200 for a woman are unnecessarily high. Slow reduction is vital, as the body has to be given the time to adapt and respond to the rejuvenatory effects of the regimen[5].

THE IMPORTANCE OF WHAT YOU EAT

Besides restricting calorie intake, the diet best suited to boost the immune defence system needs to provide a wide variety of nutrients, particularly of vitamins and minerals in their natural form. Cutting calories by simply eating less of a largely junk food diet is quite useless. Cutting calorie intake is only half the secret of long life and a healthy immune defence system. The other, vital half lies in the quality of the food that *is* consumed.

The recommended diet should be balanced, that is, organised to give you the full complement of nutrients that you require, while at the same time actively guarding against 'wasting' calories. By this is meant making certain that you do not squander the 1,000 to 2,000 calories you have per day at your disposal on nutritionally useless items. The major ones are sugar in most forms but especially white; excessive amounts of either type of fat, saturated or polyunsaturated; alcohol; and large quantities of starchy, low fibre foods such as biscuits, pasta, bread and cakes (even sugarless ones!) made from white flour.

5. *New Health* (February 1984), Teddington, UK: an adaptation from *Maximum Life Span* by Professor R. Walford, published in Britain by W. W. Norton, London

Other essential features of a diet aimed at keeping the immune defences in tip-top condition are a high-fibre and low-sodium content. We will look at the different types of fibre and their relative health-giving properties below. 'Low in sodium' means avoiding food that has sodium chloride (cooking or table salt) added to it, either in preparation or as a table condiment. Our daily requirement of sodium is in the region of 250mg, and in the West, the majority of people consume about 10g (ie, forty times in excess of requirements). High sodium diets are associated in laboratory animals with early death, and have been associated with raised blood pressure in a number of humans suffering from the condition.

An ideal dietary regimen for an adult man or woman between the ages of twenty and fifty provides a fat content of less than ten to fifteen per cent; protein, between twenty and twenty-five per cent (or ten to fifteen per cent in older people); and complex carbohydrates to make up the remaining fraction. This is a brief account of what you need and why.

Protein

Proteins are required for the continuous repair and growth processes our bodies carry out. This, of course, includes the cells and tissues of the RE and the immune defence system. The skin, too, is in constant need of protein with which to renew itself, as are the cells of the mucous membranes constituting our first-line defence system (linings of mouth, vagina, stomach and so on). It is also used to manufacture antibodies, hormones and enzymes.

When digestion takes place, the protein content of food is broken down into the simple units called amino acids of which it is composed. About twenty amino acids exist, and eight of these are labelled 'essential' because the body's requirements for them have to be met in the form of the food we take in for it cannot manufacture them for itself.

The names of the essential amino acids are: tryptophan, valine, threonine, phenylalanine, leucine, isoleucine, lysine and methionine. Most animal protein (meat, eggs, milk and milk products) contains all the essential amino acids in the required proportions, and are known as first-class protein. Vegetable and plant proteins are referred to as 'second class', because none provides all eight amino acids in the desirable proportions. All the same, there is a snag involved in getting your protein from animal products.

If you eat red meat, eggs and other animal protein sources, you inevitably take in animal (saturated) fats at the same time. A high consumption of animal fat has been shown in a multiplicity of research studies to be associated with an increased incidence of heart and arterial disease, and other circulatory problems. In addition, certain varieties of bowel cancer have been linked with a high consumption of red meat, especially beef. On the other hand, it is unwise to shun all first-class protein and depend on plant protein for your essential amino acid supply, without paying attention to two essential factors. The first is the quantity of plant (polyunsaturated) fats you consume along with them.

For a long time, the praises of plant and vegetable protein sources were sung highly, and there remains a very great deal indeed to be said in their favour. For one thing, plant and vegetable food is also our sole source of naturally occurring complex carbohydrate, and this is a very valuable food indeed. It is simply that a word of caution needs to be uttered, warning against taking in too much fat and oil from *any* source.

This is why the recommended daily allowance is as low as it is. A high intake of plant polyunsaturates has in fact been related to certain types of cancer, and simply to eat as much fat on your bread as you like, merely taking the precaution of substituting butter with a synthetic spread which claims to be 'high in polyunsaturates' is in no way a guarantee of protection from serious illness.

The second vital factor needing consideration is whether you are obtaining sufficient of the essential amino acids. The recommended daily intake of protein is 60–90g for men; and 50–65g for women. The best way to make sure that you are getting not only enough but enough of the right types, is to learn enough about the different amino acids various plant foods offer, and eat them in the combinations that *do* provide all that you need. An example of complementary proteins is the combination of beans, which are an excellent source of amino acids, yet short on methionine, together with rice, which lacks lysine supplied by the beans, yet contains ample methionine.

Other sources of protein may include fish, especially the oily types such as herring, mackerel, sardines, pilchards which also contain two essential fatty acids DHA and EPA. EPA has been shown to offer some protection against heart and circulatory disease. Three free-range eggs per week are considered by many authorities to be safe, with respect to the amount of saturated fat they supply.

Should you eat red meat?
Red meat is best avoided, and you may even find that by cutting it out of your diet, you cease to miss it and perhaps develop a dislike for it. If this is not the case, eat it only on the rare occasion – perhaps once a year – in order to indulge a strong liking for it which can amount to a craving if too rigorously denied. No-one would *recommend* the inclusion of red meat in a diet that seriously intended to strengthen the immune defence system and prolong life. Nevertheless, it is a poor heart that is never allowed to rejoice, and if one ten ounce rare fillet steak on your birthday, grilled in butter and seasoned with crushed black peppercorns and brandy, makes your day complete, then for heaven's sake go ahead and have just that!

Fibre
Fibre increases the bulk of the food in the stomach, making you feel satisfied sooner than non-bulky food. It also increases the volume of the stools, and frequency with which they are passed. Chronic constipation, generally due to a diet poor in fibre and therefore in bulk, is related by naturopaths to the accumulation of toxins in the tissues (the state of mesotrophy), and by physicians everywhere, with a number of possible disorders. A relationship between constipation and cancer of the large bowel has been shown in a number of studies, and the inclusion of high-fibre foods is considered generally to be of major importance to health and vitality.

The different types of fibre available include cellulose, gums, lignin and pectin. Cellulose comes from the cell walls of plants. It absorbs water and bulks out the motions, and helps to avoid constipation. Gums are produced by a number of plants, and help to reduce cholesterol uptake. An example is guar gum, which is a bean product. This lines the stomach and also reduces the rate at which sugar is absorbed into the blood. This is especially helpful to diabetics.

Lignin is the tough material present in root vegetables such as parsnips, carrots, swedes and turnips. It helps to give substance to food, making it more chewy and filling. Pectins are found in the soft tissues of fruit. It is thought that pectins may cut down the digestion and absorption of fat and cholesterol.

The recommended daily intake of fibre is 25–35g daily. The best sources of fibre are beans, lentils, whole grains, fresh fruit and fresh vegetables, preferably raw or very lightly cooked. Wholewheat bread and dried fruit also supply plenty of fibre. Sprinkling bran on cereals or adding it to other foods is unsatisfactory, because the phytic acid present in bran adversely affects the way we absorb calcium.

Carbohydrates

Carbohydrates fall into two classes – simple (the sugars, which in themselves provide nothing other than calories – see above); and complex (the starches – a very important source of energy). Although we are in the main advised to omit simple carbohydrates from our diet, we inevitably take some in, in combination with many of the starch or fibrous foods we eat. There is no recommended daily intake of complex carbohydrate in the UK, although it is generally recognised that this dietary constituent should make up sixty to seventy per cent of the total diet.

Certain sources of dietary sweetness need special mention. The addition of fresh fruit juice, grated fresh fruit and chopped dried fruit is often recommended for its fructose content. Molasses contains a number of useful nutrients, including iron and vitamins, and is sometimes used as a preferable form of sweetener to the white sucrose, as are the natural brown sugars, demerara and barbados.

Honey is renowned for its therapeutic properties, and of particular interest here are its natural antibiotic activities. These help fight infection without in any way compromising the strength of the body's natural defensive mechanisms. Honey is used in many natural remedies and a little may safely be added as a source of sweetness occasionally.

Good sources of complex carbohydrate include rice, grains (barley, wheat, oatmeal), wholewheat flour and its products, beans and lentils. All carbohydrates, of whatever type, are broken down by the digestive processes into simple sugar molecules. The digestion of starch starts in fact in the mouth, when food containing it is mixed with saliva. This brings it into contact with the enzyme ptyalin, which converts starch to the sugar maltose. This is further broken down in the small bowel by the enzyme maltase, into the simple sugar glucose.

Simple sugars pass through the small bowel wall into the bloodstream, and are either broken down to release energy or stored as a source of potential energy in the cells of the liver, in the form of glycogen. Too much carbohydrate is stored as fat. Vitamins, especially those in the B complex group, are required to release the energy stored in carbohydrates.

Dietary fat

Besides the polyunsaturated fat and saturated fats already mentioned, a third class exists named the monosaturates. These are present in fruit and nuts. Also, not all saturated fat is of animal origin. Two exceptions are palm oil and coconut oil. Another is hydrogenated vegetable fats present in some margarine and cooking oils.

Fat satisfies the appetite because it slows down the rate at which food is absorbed, thus providing a feeling of fullness. The fat layers also store fat-soluble vitamins, including A, D, E and K.

The essential fatty acids include linoleic acid, gammalinolenic acid (GLA) present in evening primrose oil and arachidonic acid. Linoleic acid is present in fresh, nonprocessed plant oils. The other two can be manufactured by the body, unless their synthesis is interfered with. It is generally agreed that fat ought not to constitute in excess of ten to fifteen per cent of the daily diet.

Vitamins

The water-soluble vitamins include the B complex members, and vitamin C. Unlike the fat-soluble vitamins, they cannot be stored in the body for more than a brief time, and excreted in the urine if present in excess.

Vitamins, by and large, cannot be made by the body. Certain

intestinal bacteria can synthesise vitamin K, important to the body's blood-clotting mechanism; and vitamin D is made within the skin when it is exposed to sunlight. The rest, however, have to be obtained from the diet. The reason we need vitamins is that they 'organise' or 'get going' a vast number of important biochemical reactions throughout the body, which either would not occur at all in their absence, or else would take place extremely inefficiently.

An example is vitamin B6 (pyridoxine). This has to be present for the production of red blood cells, and is vital to the immune defence system for the manufacture of antibodies. It is also necessary for the production of hydrochloric acid by the lining of the stomach, and for the proper absorption of vitamin B12.

The basic functions of the most important vitamins are as follows.

Vitamin A This keeps skin and mucous membranes (for example, lining of throat, mouth, vagina, bladder entrance) intact and healthy, and able to act as first-line defence areas. It is also necessary to vision in poor light. It is supplied by carrots, green and yellow vegetables, yellow fruit, fish oil, liver and eggs.

Vitamin B group These have many vital activities, including the metabolism of fat, carbohydrate and protein, and also the maintenance of healthy hair, skin, eyes, mucous membranes and many bodily organs, especially the liver. The main members of the vitamin B complex are vitamin B1 (thiamine), present in dried yeast, rice husks, oatmeal and peanuts; B2 (riboflavin), present in milk, liver, kidney, yeast; B3 (niacin, nicotinic acid, niacinamide), found in the white meat of poultry, whole wheat products, brewer's yeast and wheatgerm; B5 (calcium pantothenate) in crude molasses, chicken, nuts and green vegetables; B6 (pyridoxine), found in brewer's yeast, wheat bran, wheat germ, cabbage, canteloupe melons; B12 (cobalamin), present in kidney, liver, eggs and milk; and biotin (also known as coenzyme R, or vitamin H), present in nuts, egg yolk, brown rice and many fruits.

Other B complex members include choline (egg yolks, offal, yeast, green leafy vegetables); folic acid (dark green leafy vegetables, carrots, avocado pears, dark rye flour and pumpkins); inositol (liver, brewer's yeast, unrefined molasses and dried lima beans); and PABA (para-amino benzoic acid), found in liver, heart or kidneys, whole grains, rice, bran and molasses.

Vitamin C Of great importance to the body in helping to protect it from infectious illnesses. It also promotes the healing of wounds, and strengthens connective tissue. More will be said about the importance of vitamin C to the immune defence mechanism in the next chapter. This vitamin is found in rich supply in citrus fruit, berries, green and yellow vegetables, potatoes and tomatoes.

Vitamin D This helps us retain the right amounts of calcium and phosphorus in the bloodstream, and encourages calcium to be absorbed, thus strengthening bones and teeth. The best natural sources include fish liver oils, tuna, herring, sardines, milk and dairy products.

Vitamin E This is present in the outer membranes of all body cells. It keeps these in a healthy state, and protects vitamin A from being destroyed. It also facilitates the body's use of unsaturated fats, and of GLA (gammalinolenic acid), an essential fatty acid. Good sources of this vitamin include soya beans, wheat germ, vegetable oil, broccoli, bean sprouts, spinach and wholewheat.

Vitamin K This helps prevent internal bleeding and haemorrhages. It also helps to reduce excessively heavy menstrual blood loss, and helps the blood clotting mechanism to function properly. It can be found in yoghurt, egg yolk, safflower oil, fish liver oils and green leafy vegetables.

Minerals

The plants we eat absorb minerals from the soil, and provide us with our best dietary source. The most important minerals to health include potassium, calcium, magnesium, phosphorus and iron. With the exception of iron, these make up a great part of the skeletal and connective tissue framework of the body, and are especially evident in bones, teeth, muscle fibres, nerves and the plasma, the fluid fraction of the blood in which the blood cells are transported.

Minerals are also part of the molecular structure of many vital body chemicals such as enzymes, vitamins and hormones. The trace element chromium, for instance, is part of the structure of insulin, the hormone that maintains a normal blood glucose level and which is deficient or defective in diabetics. Another example is iron, present in the haemoglobin molecule, the red pigment in the cytoplasm of red cells responsible for transporting oxygen around the bloodstream from the lungs to the tissues.

Certain minerals work reciprocally. Calcium and phosphorus, for example, always have to 'balance' one another, and an increased intake of, say, phosphorus into the body increases the need for calcium. A varied and balanced diet containing a high proportion of fresh fruit and vegetables and their freshly squeezed juices, pulses and nuts, normally ensures that the majority of people take sufficient minerals not to need supplements. However, stress, fatigue, and the effects of pollution, the contraceptive pill, antibiotics, alcohol, caffeine and other drugs, and food-production techniques that introduce phosphate fertilisers into our systems, can upset our mineral balance and require supplementation.

Rich sources of magnesium include bran, wheatgerm, Brazil nuts, peanuts, millet and oatmeal. Calcium is found in milk and milk products, spinach, parsley, salmon, dried figs and beans, watercress and almonds.

Potassium is supplied by blackstrap molasses, yeast extract, bran, citrus fruit, bananas, tomatoes, wheatgerm and dried apricots and peaches.

Phosphorus is provided by meat, poultry, fish, eggs, nuts, seeds, and whole grains.

Iron comes from meat and offal, blackstrap molasses, spinach, watercress, nuts fresh yeast, egg yolk, wheatgerm and millet.

FASTING TIPS

Why not treat yourself to the benefits of a short fast from time to time? Alternatively, you may wish to follow Professor Walford's undernutrition regimen for the benefit to your immune defences, by means of doing without food entirely for a day or so every week. Here is the best way to go about either.

Choose two consecutive days when you are able to rest as and when you want to, or at least have as few demands made upon you as your lifestyle allows. For most people, this is a weekend. Prepare the day before, by avoiding alcohol, cigarettes, junk snacks, coffee, tea, fried food and red meat. (Hopefully, you are not a smoker in the first place, and are by now aware of the foods to avoid anyway.)

On day one of your two-day fast, drink freshly squeezed fruit or vegetable juice (see below, 'Your Healthy Diet'), half a pint four times daily. Of particular use to your immune defence system, are carrot, apple, cabbage and tomato juice. I would recommend that half your daily intake of juice be carrot, and the rest made up as you feel inclined. Certain mixtures are delicious. Apple and carrot go nicely together, and so do cabbage and tomato juice.

In addition, drink as much mineral water as you want – this really helps to release toxins and aids the kidneys in flushing waste materials from your system. In the evening, before going to bed, eat a small bunch of grapes (about 100g), well rinsed to remove any toxic spray that they may be carrying.

On the second day, take half a pint of carrot juice in the morning, half a pint of mixed carrot and apple at lunch time, two large apples at tea time, and six ounces of grapes before retiring.

If you like, you can start off each day with either a cup of herbal tea (lemon verbena is nice, especially with a thick slice of lemon floating in it), or with a mug of very hot water to which you have added the juice of half a lemon or half a grapefruit.

On the day after your two fasting days, make sure that you reintroduce your normal diet gradually. Eat fruit and muesli or yoghurt for breakfast, a salad for lunch, and perhaps some lightly cooked fish with some stir-fried vegetables, followed by fruit and plain, live yoghurt in the evening.

YOUR HEALTHY DIET

If the foods recommended in this chapter as especially healthy, are quite different from those you have been used to eating, changing your entire approach to shopping, cooking and eating may seem a daunting prospect. In fact, most wholefood cookery is simple and straightforward, and requires little in the way of culinary equipment and skill that the average adult does not already possess.

The main exception to this is an electric juicer. This item is in fact worth its weight in cut diamonds, if you are really interested in boosting your immune defences. The juice of fresh, live plants as mentioned above is a marvellous source of concentrated plant sugars, vitamins, minerals, plant protein, trace elements (ie, the minerals we require in minute quantities) and enzymes. Buy such a juicer, and you will be amazed at the variety of vegetable and fruit juices you can think up, combine and enjoy.

As a rough guideline to following a healthy diet, here are some ideas to start you off.

Breakfast Live yoghurt, homemade or health food shop muesli without added sugar, fresh fruit, wholewheat scone or bap with scraping of fat and some yeast extract if liked. Glass of fresh juice or cup of herb tea.

Mid-morning snack Piece of fresh fruit, wholewheat or whole-grain biscuit without added sugar, piece of dried fruit, for example figs or dates.

Lunch Large salad, with plenty of green, leafy vegetables. Avoid expensive and tasteless lettuce in the off-season, and opt for Chinese cabbage leaves, grated green or white cabbage, grated carrot, finely chopped celery, chopped red cabbage or cress as the basis of your meal. Add protein in the form of low fat cheese, a boiled egg, a handful of mixed unsalted nuts, or some cold cooked rice or whole grain. Barley cooked with a little vegetable extract and a handful of herbs, strained, allowed to cool and added to such a salad, is very pleasant, as are buckwheat, millet and brown rice.

Add interest to the salad with a few choice extras – some sliced avocado pear, a couple of tomatoes, a green, red or yellow pepper, some sunflower or pumpkin seeds. (These are delicious, and certainly should not be thought of as exclusively parrot food!)

Follow by fruit or yoghurt.

Evening meal (This is exchangeable with lunch if required) Eat vegetarian sometimes, basing your meal on rice or wholewheat pasta, lentils, dried pulses or freshly cooked vegetables. Steam, briefly boil or stir fry your food in preference to roasting or frying. Always use minimal fat, and choose a cold-pressed, non-hydrogenated oil such as the virgin olive oil available in health food shops. It is expensive, but of very high quality and lasts for ages if you use it sparingly.

Add protein to non-vegetarian meals with steamed or foil-baked fish, some offal occasionally, poultry, low- and medium-fat cheeses. Use flavourings such as fresh and dried herbs, and garlic, liberally. Include a scattering of chopped fresh nuts and a handful of seeds wherever possible. A healthy way of thickening soups without having recourse to a classic roux, is to add the 'waste' fibre you obtain in the collecting chamber of your juicer when you make vegetable juice. This is an excellent source of natural fibre and adds no calories to the dish.

Finish your meal with fresh fruit, yoghurt, fruit ambers or crumbles made with wholewheat flour and vegetable fat, home-made fruit sorbets and icecreams, or fresh fruit salad. If you want a really healthy equivalent to double cream, try Greek strained yoghurt, available now in most large supermarkets. It is thick and very rich-tasting, yet relatively low in calories and saturated fat.

6 Dietary Supplements for Health

Although the last chapter went into some detail about what constitutes healthy eating, we have not yet touched upon the subject of dietary supplements. It may be hard to believe that anyone who follows a truly healthy diet could possibly require a supplementary supply of vitamins, minerals, trace elements, amino acids and glandular extracts as well. It remains a fact, though, that these are an essential tool if you are really determined to boost your immune defence system to the optimal possible level of functioning.

Here are the reasons. Anyone who has ever been on a calorie-restricted slimming diet knows what a time-consuming task it can be to note down the calorific value of every single item of food and drink consumed in a day. The temptation grows to give up the whole enterprise as an impossible job when, despite carrying your book of food energy values round with you as though your life depended on it, you *still* get faced with insoluble problems that the composers of slimming diets never seem to think of.

You can be invited out to dinner, for example, and while you may have every intention of ordering a grilled fillet steak and side salad, followed by fresh fruit, you end up being persuaded to try the duck in orange sauce or salmon koulibiak. Trying to calculate just how much sugar or honey the orange sauce contained, or how much fat was used to make the koulibiac's delectable pastry, is so mind-boggling, that your most likely reaction is to shrug your shoulders, decide to start dieting again 'tomorrow', and console yourself with a huge slice of coffee meringue gâteau (with added whipped cream) for dessert.

Imagine, therefore, the difficulty involved in making certain that you are including sufficient magnesium, calcium, potassium, iron and trace elements in your daily diet. The problems are almost insurmountable, and the only sensible *workable* solution is to eat the healthiest diet, including as much fresh, raw fruit and vegetables as you can, and supplement this with tried and tested nutritional supplements.

Another reason for adopting this approach is that a number of the supplements now known to benefit the immune defence system, are present in incalculable quantities in food, and it is impossible to know how much of them you are taking or, indeed, if you are actually taking them at all. They are available only as nutritional supplements which, to be effective, have to have been prepared under very carefully controlled conditions.

VITAMINS AND MINERALS

For confirmation of our very real need for such supplements, we can refer again to Professor Royal Walford's experiments into boosting the strength of the immune defence system, outlined in the last chapter. Not only did the animals on calorie-restricted diets remain younger and live longer, providing direct evidence of the health and well-being of the immune defence system. They also remained outstandingly free from degenerative diseases generally, and far less likely than their freely fed counterparts to succumb to common complaints, including infectious illnesses.

Confirmation of Professor Walford's findings has been established by the repetition of his experiments by groups of gerontologists (specialists in the ageing process), immunologists and immuno-gerontologists all over the world. The results show that the secret of keeping the immune defences in a superbly healthy state is the combination of calorie restriction with a diet of very high nutritional standard. In order to ensure all the vital nutrients are being taken, scientists in this field recommend a daily multipurpose vitamin and mineral supplement, and as many other factors as have been shown by observation to boost our immune resources.

Inadequate diet and illness

Much is known about the 'reverse side of the coin', that is, the strong correlation between malnutrition and a greatly increased risk of succumbing to diseases generally. To take susceptibility to infections as a case in point, the following effects of malnutrition are especially relevant. The production of interferon is inhibited, and the amount of 'complement', the protein which works in conjunction with antibodies, is reduced. The antibody response to attenuated measles and rubella vaccine is reduced, and the tonsils, which are thought to produce white blood cells which destroy pathogenic bacteria in the mouth and throat, become smaller. Moreover, the antibacterial substances (enzymes) present in sweat, tears and peritoneal fluid (the fluid within the abdominal cavity) are decreased. In fact, the relationship between adequate nutrition and protection from disease and infection, is strongly established and indisputable.

We also saw in the last chapter, the proportions of carbodydrate, fat and protein which our diets should contain, and what we need in the way of vitamins and minerals. Our basic requirements of these should be met by combining a healthy diet with the daily 'all-purpose' vitamin and mineral supplement mentioned above. We are going to look in closer detail here at those particular nutrients needed to have specific significance to the immune defence system. In some cases, we will need to take extra quantities of these in supplementary form, in addition to that which is already being supplied by our diet and multivitamin/mineral pill.

The antioxidants

Professor Walford attaches a great deal of importance in the preservation of a healthy and vigorous immune system to a group of substances known as antioxidants. These substances and their activities in the body were not discovered by him and have in fact been known about for a long time, much research having been devoted to them. He is convinced that antioxidants are a vital dietary supplement when the aim in view is anti-ageing, reduced suscepti-bility to degenerative and auto-immune diseases, and an increased resistance to all the factors, including pathogenic organisms, that deplete and injure our immunological response.

The most powerful antioxidants found in food include vitamins C,

E and A, some of the B complex, the trace element selenium and the sulphur-containing amino acids cysteine and methionine. These, and the enzymes superoxide dismutase (SOD), catalase and glutathione peroxidase, act as free radical scavengers. This means that they can degrade, neutralise or detoxify free radicals.

Free radicals are molecules that possess an extra electrical charge. They are produced within the cells of the body naturally, by the oxidative (energy-providing) processes that take place there. They are also formed as a result of taking in rancid fats and oils and other pollutants, and by the invasion of our bodies by chemical and environmental toxins.

Professor Walford has coined an apt name for these free radicals – he refers to them as 'great white sharks in the biochemical sea'. They oxidise and damage tissue, particularly the membranes of cells, thereby forming more free radicals. They interact with polyunsaturated fats which results ultimately in the cross-linking of bodily proteins, lipids (cellular fats) and DNA (deoxyribonucleic acid, part of our genetic code material present in the nuclei of all cells). The physical effect of these activities at biochemical level is that the affected structures become rigid and immobile, and their ability to function deteriorates. These are the same ageing characteristics as those that affect their human hosts.

Dr Denham Harman, at the University of Nebraska, another well-known biogerontologist, is convinced that supplementing the diet with the opponents of free radicals (ie, free radical scavengers as mentioned above), substantially increases survival and has a very highly beneficial effect upon the immune defence system. It is important to use supplementation to achieve this benefit since, as pointed out previously, it is vital to know that one is taking in a sufficient amount of these valuable substances on a day-to-day basis.

Professor Walford's personal daily antioxidant supplement intake includes the following:

Vitamin E	600 IU
Vitamin C	1000 mg
Selenium	160 mcg
BHT	150 mg
Ascorbyl palmitate*	600 mg

Bioflavinoids	300 mg
Cysteine	300 mg
Methionine	300 mg

(*Ascorbyl palmitate is the fat-soluble form of vitamin C. It has potent antioxidant properties and it penetrates into cellular compartments not reached by the ordinary water-soluble form. It is included in some maximum life formulas and enhancers).

Vitamin C   This is much more than simply an antioxidant. It helps to protect the body against invading toxins, bacteria and viruses. It can fight stress-induced symptoms such as over-stimulation of the adrenal glands and excessive protein breakdown which predispose to infection. It has a beneficial effect in test-tube cultures containing macrophages, increasing their action of engulfing and destroying invading organisms, and it has also been shown to stimulate the production of interferon. It also reduces the blood cholesterol level, and may possibly extend the lives of certain cancer patients.

As long ago as the 1950s, the American research scientist and physician Dr Frederick Klenner, who is famous for his work with vitamin C and has been taking it in megadoses for over thirty years, discovered that this vitamin had a non-specific action upon viruses and was deadly to all types. At the time of Dr Klenner's discovery, nothing was known about interferon. However, in 1970, Dr Robert Cathart hypothesised that vitamin C was involved in the synthesis of interferon, since the action of this substance is to prevent the entry of viruses into the cells where they breed and multiply.

A research paper produced by Dr Benjamin V. Siegel of the Health and Medical Department, University of Oregon, confirms that vitamin C ascorbate greatly increases the production of interferon in animals. Mice receiving vitamin C supplements in their drinking water were found subsequently to produce greater than usual amounts of interferon when exposed to viral infection. Scandinavian research has since confirmed Dr Siegel's findings, using human tissue.

It is an interesting fact that humans are among the three or four animals that do not manufacture their own vitamin C. It seems that we have all the biochemical requirements for the process with the exception of a single liver enzyme. A number of scientists believe that humans suffer some type of mutation (change in the genetic coding material) which causes this state of affairs, and maintains us in a mild state of scurvy.

Considering the importance of vitamin C to the immune system, we should most certainly take it as a supplement. The usual daily recommended dose for adults is 1,000–3,000mg, and doses very many times this quantity have been used, sometimes with success, in the treatment of cancer. It has also been suggested that very high doses of vitamin C might deal effectively with AIDS in its early stages. The newer forms of vitamin C are probably more efficient than some of the longer established varieties, for example the time-release type, and the vitamin C powders with mineral ascorbates.

Bioflavinoids   These are plant pigments. They occur in particularly high concentration in the pith of grapefruit, oranges and tangerines, and in lesser amounts in all raw plant food. They were discovered in 1936 by Nobel prize winner Albert Szent-Gyorgyi, the Hungarian biochemist who first isolated and identified vitamin C.

In plants themselves, the bioflavinoids help to prevent disease, and they perform the same role in humans. Two members of the group[6], nobiletin and a closely related substance have strong anti-inflammatory powers. Others, either on their own or in combination, actively combat pathogenic bacteria, viruses and fungi. Nobiletin and tangeretin boost the activity of a group of enzymes called the mixed-function oxidases whose job it is to rid the body of drugs, heavy metals and the unburnt hydrocarbons in car exhausts. As we saw in the early part of this book, all of these toxins are deleterious to health in general and to the immune defence system in particular.

Indirectly, these two bioflavinoids are also cancer-preventing, as Leslie and Susannah Kenton point out in *Raw Energy*. Bioflavinoids generally seem to be most active when an organism is under particular stress. They are thought, therefore, to have a specifically homoeostatic function, tending to right the bodily functions that become disturbed when subjected to illnesses and intensely stressful situations, including emergencies. Bioflavinoids are usually available as a dietary supplement in conjunction with vitamin C.

6. Kenton, L. and S. *Raw Energy* Century Publishing, page 62

One of the reasons for the effect of the bioflavinoids is that they inhibit the destruction by oxidation of vitamin C, and increase its action. High doses of C need to be accompanied by sufficient dietary fatty acids, as well as zinc and vitamins B6 (pyridoxine) and E.

Excess vitamin C is excreted from the blood in the urine within three to four hours, so the best way to maintain maximum blood levels is to take it in small amounts every few hours rather than in a large dose once every twenty-four hours.

Vitamin E The particular area of antioxidant activity of this vitamin, which is fat-soluble, is the membrane of cells. Here it scavenges for free radicals, protecting the membrane from injury. In large doses, it has been found to decrease the rate at which the brown-coloured pigment characteristic of the ageing process accumulates in the skin.

SOD and BHT SOD by contrast, exerts its beneficial influence within the cell fluid, while BHT, the food preservative, was found by Dr Denham Harman to be one of the most effective agents in increasing the average lifespan in long-lived strains of mice. The increase was as high as thirty per cent and, even more important, indicates that even animals with an inherited tendency to longevity can benefit from the use of antioxidants. Mice with naturally shorter lifespans had their lives increased by an average of forty-five per cent.

Selenium This is one of the most important minerals in stimulating healthy immune function. In *Selenium as Food and Medicine*, Dr Richard Passwater reports that selenium has improved the protective level of the immune system by a factor of twenty to thirty. Studies from Colorado State University show that dietary supplementation with selenium at levels in excess of the recommended nutritional requirements enhanced both primary and secondary immune responses. This element contributes to the formation of interferon and is believed to play a direct role in macrophage production.

It was discovered in the Soviet Union in 1972, that when selenium and vitamin E were given along with vaccine, more antibodies were produced than were normally evoked by the vaccine alone.

However, this only occurs when the vitamin and mineral are given together with one another. Selenium given alone boosts antibody production slightly, but vitamin E used by itself had no effect at all on this function. A substance known as co-enzyme Q, which will be discussed further on in this chapter, also augments antibody production following vaccine administration, provided it is used in the presence of selenium.

Cysteine and methionine   The amino acids cysteine and methionine, present in much protein food, are chemical precursors of the amino acid glutathione which is used by the body to combine with and eliminate toxic foreign substances. Fifty-three per cent of cysteine-fed mice were alive at eighteen months compared with none in the control experiment in which this particular protective ability was being tested. Cysteine has to be taken with double quantities of vitamin C to inhibit the formation of cystine, which can lead to the formation of renal (kidney) stones. It is believed that antioxidants used in combination with one another are more effective than the sum of their parts. This is known as a synergistic effect.

Vitamin A   This was the first fat-soluble vitamin to be discovered. It is a valuable antioxidant, and is also known as the anti-infection vitamin. Blood levels of this vitamin fall when infection is present, and a five-year study has confirmed that the ease with which people succumb to infectious illnesses is inversely proportional to the levels of both vitamin C and vitamin A in their blood. In addition, the presence of vitamin A reduced the length of the infectious illnesses suffered.

Vitamin A is manufactured in the body from its precursor betacarotene, obtained from carrots and green leafy vegetables. Besides its antioxidant activity, which protects the body cells from free radical trauma, this vitamin is also involved with determining the antibody specific immunity level.

A further way in which vitamin A helps to protect us from invasion by toxins and pathogens, is at the level of our first-line defences. When a deficiency exists, the health of the skin and the integrity and function of the mucous membranes lining various sites of the body, are badly impaired. Instead of dead cells being cast off in the normal manner from the outermost layers, and being constantly renewed from healthily growing cell layers below, dead cells accumulate. The cells which normally secrete mucous to produce essential lubrication, are no longer able to do so, and the affected areas become highly suitable breeding grounds for harmful bacteria.

Laboratory experiments involving mice which were exposed to two types of bacteria, and to a fungus, showed that the animals which had been treated with vitamin A survived from five to twenty times longer than the untreated controls in all cases.

It has also been reported that large daily doses of vitamin A build up immunity against environmental pollutants. Other activities include the prevention of night blindness and hypersensitivity to light; protection against sunburn and against the ageing effects of exposure to sun, wind and rain upon the skin; reduction of susceptibility to respiratory problems, including head colds, sinusitis, asthma, bronchitis and ear infections. It can also be useful in the treatment of certain cases of cystic fibrosis.

Care has to be taken not to take too much vitamin A, however. While the effects of a deficiency of this vitamin are troublesome and serious, the effects of vitamin A toxicity are no less so. The white blood cells contain digestive enzymes enclosed within small discrete areas of their cytoplasm (organelles) named lysosomes. Too much vitamin A causes the membranes enclosing the lysosomes to rupture, with the result that the digestive enzymes are released. The affected cells and their surrounding tissues, as well as extracellular structures, then come under attack from the enzymes.

This damage is thought to be the explanation for the spontaneous fractures and other lesions that occur in severe cases of vitamin A intoxication resulting from chronic excessive intake. Other symptoms are bone pain, abnormal appearance of the skin, diarrhoea and vomiting, weakness and convulsions. Vitamin A is stored within the liver, and having to store excessive quantities of it causes the liver to become inflamed. Protein is needed to remove stored vitamin A from the liver cells, and a protein deficiency can prevent the release and essential transport of this vitamin.

Some individuals are more susceptible to the effects of vitamin A toxicity than others. Deficiency of this vitamin is so deleterious, and the benefits from taking regular supplements are so desirable, that it is well worth taking it on a daily basis providing the dosage limits are not exceeded. The usual dose recommended for an adult is within the range of 10,000 to 25,000 IU daily. Qualified health specialists may recommend large amounts, but these should be taken under such expert guidance only, and the effects frequently monitored.

B complex vitamins   Certain of the B vitamins have an antioxidant effect, and several of them are important to the immune defence system in other ways. A deficiency of pantothenic acid (vitamin B5) severely reduces immune antibody response, and the same is true of both vitamin B6 (pyridoxine) and folic acid.

All three are also particularly good stress fighters, especially folic aid and pyridoxine. B6 is required for cell multiplication and synthesis. White blood cells in B6-deficient animals respond in a defensive context only half as well as those from healthy animals. It is also believed that B6 deficiency might reduce the production of macrophages.

A further relevant fact about the importance of pyridoxine to the immune defence system, is that it has been found to be essential in pregnant animals for the normal development of the thymus gland in the developing offspring. This gland in the upper chest is responsible for converting stem cells from the bone marrow into fully fledged T cells. The B lymphocytes also develop from stem cells, but reach their stage of maturity as fully developed B lymphocytes within the bone marrow itself.

Deficiencies of vitamin B1 (thiamine), B2 (riboflavin), niacin (B3) and biotin (coenzyme R) have a moderate effect upon antibody production.

Minerals
We have already looked at the necessity for selenium, and its antioxidant properties to the healthy functioning of our immune defence system. Other non-antioxidant minerals are also vital in a number of ways, and we will take a brief look at them.

Zinc   This is believed to be absolutely essential to immune defence function. More than seventy enzymes in the body are dependent upon the presence of zinc in order to function, and this metal is also important in countering viral attack. It is also essential to the healthy growth of cells, and to the biosynthesis of the nucleic acids RNA and DNA. In addition, a deficiency of zinc causes the thymus gland to atrophy (shrivel up), resulting in greatly increased susceptibility to infections. Research into the addition of non-toxic levels of zinc to tissue cultures infected with a strain of virus, showed that the further progressive development of the infectious viruses was at once inhibited.

Calcium   This has a multiplicity of biochemical functions within the body, and its effects are very important both to the overall response to stress and in defence against viral attack. Calcium is required in greater quantities than any other mineral. Women have a special need for it to help guard against osteoporosis (bone thinning) that can occur as a result of low oestrogen levels at the time of the menopause and thereafter. Calcium levels are also depleted by smoking, so cigarette smokers have an even greater need for this mineral than others. Menopausal women who are also smokers have the greatest need of all.

Vitamin C is also more efficient when taken with calcium. Among the key nutrients necessary for optimal calcium utilisation are vitamins A, C, D and the B complex; and the minerals magnesium, potassium and phosphorus. The ratio of calcium to magnesium should be two parts of calcium to one of magnesium when they are taken together. Dolomite, a naturally occurring mineral, is a common source of calcium as a dietary supplement and has the advantage of supplying calcium and magnesium together and in the correct ratio. However, the advice given in this book is basically to take mineral supplements in their chelated ('key-lated'), that is, in their most digestible, and assimilable, forms.

Chelated minerals   When minerals are chelated, they are combined molecularly with an amino acid. This is normally a process which the body performs for itself, but the process is inefficient in many people, with the result that only ten per cent of unchelated minerals taken as supplements will be assimilated and used as intended. When minerals are taken in the chelated form, the assimilation is between three and five times more efficient.

The ratio of calcium to phosphorus in the diet should be 1:1. However, the inadvertent ingestion of phosphate fertilisers used in non-organic farming can upset the delicate balance between the two minerals, with the result that calcium leaches out of the bones.

Potassium   This is the most important intracellular mineral, and is to the cell interior what sodium is to the cell's external fluid environment, the blood plasma and tissue fluid. Its particular relevance to the immune response is that it acts as an ascorbate transporter, facilitating the passage of vitamin C through the cell membrane.

Trace elements   Not a great deal is as yet known about the relationship between trace elements and the immune defence system. However, in the natural treatment of cancer, in which a diet with a very high content of raw fruit and vegetables, and raw juices, plays a vital part, trace elements are taken in in abundance, together with the concentrated and naturally occurring vitamins, minerals, enzymes, sugars and proteins which the plants and their juices contain.

The Gerson cancer diet, for example, prescribes ten 225g glasses a day of fresh carrot, apple and green vegetable juice. It is believed that the sum total of the nutrients in raw juices and plant foods, helps to render cancer cells more vulnerable to attack and liquidation by the body's immune defence system.

A further phenomenon involving our immune defences which it is pertinent to mention here because of its connection with raw foods, is digestive leucocytosis. A diet that includes a high proportion of cooked and processed foods, gradually robs the body of essential nutrients and weakens the immune defence system. In turn, the body's resistance to stress, fatigue, diseases and infectious illnesses becomes impaired.

Research carried out in the 1930s by Paul Kouchakoff at the Institute of Clinical Chemistry in Lausanne, indicates that the body recognises cooked or processed food as harmful in a comparable way to the manner in which it picks out 'self' from 'non-self' when encountering an antigen. Correspondingly, the defence mechanisms try to eliminate it. The white blood cells (leucocytes) hasten to the scene of the invasion (the intestine) as soon as cooked food enters the mouth, an occurrence known as digestive leucocytosis.

This does not occur when raw food is eaten, and eating some raw food before a cooked meal, prevents its happening at all. The probable explanation[7] for this, is that certain aromatic and other substances in raw foods that are destroyed by cooking, facilitate the easy digestion and assimilation of the food which contains them, without the necessity for wakening of the body's defence mechanisms.

The significance of this finding is believed to be that, by repeating the digestive leucocytosis phenomenon, the body gradually exhausts the resources of the immune defence system. Raw foods do not interfere with the functioning of the white cells and the protective mechanisms they represent, and leave them free to defend the body in full strength wherever required.

Leslie and Susannah Kenton suggest in *Raw Energy* that every meal containing a cooked dish, should be preceded by some raw food. A small, fresh salad is suitable, or some raw fruit.

OTHER NUTRITIONAL SUPPLEMENTS———

DMG

A recently recognised nutritional supplement of benefit to the body's immune responses is the nutrient DMG (N, N-dimethylglycine)[8]. Recent research has shown that this substance is of direct nutritional benefit to the immune defence system, that it stimulates the immune response, and that it may enhance the immune response in diabetics and in people suffering from sickle cell anaemia. Other names for DMG are pangamic acid, and calcium pangamate (Russian formula).

Research into this substance started in the USSR in the 1960s, and interest in it has spread at research level into the USA, Japan, Germany and Australia. It is related to choline, a member of the B vitamin complex, and it is the smallest molecular configuration to have vitamin B activity. It was at one time confused with what is now known as vitamin B15, but in fact DMG is not a vitamin, in that its

7. Kenton, L. and S. *Raw Energy* Century Publishing, page 41
8. *Nutrition News* (no. 98), Felmore Ltd (Health Publications). 1 Lamberts Road, PO Box 1, Tunbridge Wells TN2 3EQ, UK

absence from the diet does not produce a deficiency state.

It is generally considered to be a metabolic enhancer, which has been defined as a 'food substance whose *absence* in the diet does not produce symptoms of disease, but whose *presence* in the diet in optimal quantities can improve physical and mental performance, especially under stressful situations' (Dr Meduski, Nutritional Research Laboratory, the University of Southern California Medical School).

The human body produces DMG from choline, and it is also provided in small quantities in food. As a nutritional supplement, Dr Meduski recommends 100mg daily for an average adult. Double blind clinical trials into the mode of function of DMG, indicate that it enhances both antibody production (humoral immunity) and cellular immunity, using less than 100mg daily. The immunologist Dr Charles Graber's research into this, carried out at the University of South Carolina School of Medicine, shows that DMG significantly stimulates B cells to produce much higher antibody responses and also promotes T cell and macrophage activity.

Dr Richard Passwater's comment upon these findings is that 'while other nutrients have been shown to augment antibody response *or* cellular immunity, this is the first report of any nutrient (or drug) enhancing both aspects of the immune system'.

Raw glandular extracts

Raw thymus gland extracts (and extracts of many other bodily glands) can now be prepared in a way that involves no high temperatures that might damage the delicate glandular tissue used. Specific immune defence reactions are depressed in poorly nourished people, probably in part through a direct effect upon the thymus gland, the spleen and the lymph nodes.

It is thought that 'raw' thymus may be beneficial in stimulating the action of the thymus gland. With age, the thymus tends to atrophy and to decline in hormone activity, particularly between the ages of 25 and 45. This fact may be responsible for the decrease in immune capacity that accompanies the ageing process. Certainly, thymus gland transplants from young mice have successfully rejuvenated the immune response in old mice.

Dr Hans Selye, renowned for his work into the effects of stress, explains that proteins are drawn from the thymus and lymph glands when stress levels are raised. Severe stress causes the thymus gland to shrink even more rapidly than is usual, demonstrating the body's need to draw upon its resources. This gland is also markedly atrophied in malnourished people.

Raw thymus glandular extract is thought to have the ability to stimulate and nourish the activity of the actual thymus gland, by providing it with all the specific nutrients it needs for cellular replacement and reconstruction. In particular, these include hormones, amino acids, and other regulating factors. The supplement tablets consist of concentrated thymus tissue taken from animal thymus material. They have caused a great deal of controversial discussion because the chief criticism against them is that any useful material they contained would beyond doubt be broken down and digested in the alimentary tract.

Nevertheless, there is ample evidence to show that oral glandular therapy *does* work. Giving extracts of the whole gland rather than administering specific hormones such as insulin in the case of diabetes, is a safer approach in many human conditions because it is gentler and a great deal more balanced. Side-effects are not a problem.

A well-known researcher into this and related questions, W. A. Hemmings, has suggested that a fair proportion of the food protein molecules provided by our food do in fact evade breakdown by proteolytic enzymes. It is also known that up to twenty per cent of the food proteins which have left the bloodstream and entered the tissues, keep their original characteristics as complex animal proteins. There is also clinical evidence that carefully prepared glandular extracts do in fact have a significant therapeutic effect explainable in terms of their hormone, enzyme, essential fatty acid and prostaglandin content.

Thymosin and co-enzyme Q

Other approaches to overcoming the problem of thymus gland degeneration and concomitant decrease in the vitality and efficiency of the immune defence system, are being looked at. They have included the administration of thymosin (the thymus hormone) to ageing laboratory animals, and the treatment of elderly animals requiring regeneration with a substance known as co-enzyme Q. In the case of the thymosin-treated animals, there was a life extension of between fifty and one hundred per cent when compared with the control group. This was because the function of the T cells remained normal, due to the stimulation and control exerted by the exogenous thymosin.

The experimental administration of both thymosin and co-enzyme Q has had as its primary objective the extension of the healthy human lifespan. In this book, we are concerned less with life extension and all that that implies, than with simply boosting the immune defence system in order that we can remain healthy and infection-resistant. Nevertheless, retarding the ageing process and increasing the body's resistance to cancer and degenerative disease processes, is an inseparable part of the function of healthy immune defences, and it is not possible to focus upon one aspect of immune defence function without some of the spotlight being automatically trained upon its other aspects as well.

Few people would probably consider that thymosin administration or co-enzyme Q were among the best ways of, for example, avoiding the common cold or influenza. All the same, benefiting one immune function will inevitably benefit others, and as these techniques at the time of writing are still largely in their investigative stage, I am mentioning them from the interest point of view, and for what they could come to mean to us in the future.

Co-enzyme Q has been called 'a vital link in the metabolic machinery of living cells'. It appears to stimulate the mitochondria in cell nuclei, the minute 'power stations' that provide the energy for cellular activities. In laboratory tests comparing the ratios of liver, spleen and thymus weight to body weight in both young and old mice, the ratios of both liver and spleen weight to body weight remained more or less constant, but the ratio of thymus weight to body weight decreased significantly with age. This thymus gland weight decline was accompanied by steeply falling levels of co-enzyme Q activity.

Humans experience a similar reduction in co-enzyme Q levels as the thymus gland atrophies. Animal tests show that the introduction of co-enzyme Q into the body in supplement form increases resistance to disease. Studies so far reported upon suggest that the administration of co-enzyme Q as a supplement to restore falling blood levels of this enzyme may well reverse the age-related suppression of immunological responsiveness. In other words, it seems that giving co-enzyme Q as a dietary supplement is likely to restore immune function and simultaneously postpone the onset of the ageing process.

Evening primrose oil

The oil of the seeds of the evening primrose flower is thought very likely to possess anti-ageing properties. The ageing process at biochemical level is one of the factors that inhibits the trans-formation of dietary cis-linoleic acid (an essential fatty acid present in safflower and sunflower seed oil) into gamma-linoleic acid (GLA), a necessary preliminary step in the series of reactions that ultimately produce prostaglandins.

Prostaglandins are hormone-like substances, and both harmful and vital types exist. The variety made from cis-linoleic acid referred to here, are of a type known as the E1 group and these are vital to the second-by-second control of a wide variety of cellular metabolic processes taking place throughout the body. One of the functions of these E1 prostaglandins is to control in part the immune response. Others are the inhibition of blood clot formation, and facilitation of the process by which hormonal 'messages' are transported to the nuclei of cells.

Evening primrose oil contains GLA. This means that the problem of non-conversion of cis-linoleic acid into GLA is overcome when this supplement is taken on a daily basis, and the manufacture of prostaglandins can proceed forthwith.

It follows from this and other information, obtained over the last decade or so from intensive research into the biochemistry of essential fatty acids and prostaglandin formation, that the ageing process has a directly deleterious effect upon the healthy function of the immune defence system, at a biochemical as well as a cellular level. Other factors besides the ageing process known to affect adversely cis-linoleic acid conversion include diabetes, viral infec-tions, prolonged stress (the presence of large amounts of adrenaline and noradrenaline in the bloodstream inhibits the manufacture of GLA), the inclusion in the diet of large amounts of saturated animal fats, and the presence in food of 'trans' linoleic acid.

Trans-linoleic acid is a useless form of the useful cis-linoleic acid from which GLA is made. It is formed when cis-linoleic acid in plant oil is processed and hydrogenated during the manufacture of margarine and similar products, or when cooking oil containing cis-linoleic acid is heated to high temperatures. Trans-linoleic acid is not only incapable of conversion into GLA; it actually possesses antivitamin properties which prevent any available cisform of this essential fatty acid from being so converted.

CELL THERAPY

T and B cell therapy is used to treat patients suffering from immune suppression. There are a number of instances in which this suppression can arise, one familiar one being as a side-effect of treatment for cancer, and for auto-immune diseases such as rheumatoid arthritis.

The T and B cells (ie, T lymphocytes and B lymphocytes) are taken from the patient while the immune system is functioning normally. One could argue that no patient suffering from cancer or from an auto-immune condition has a normal immune system. All the same, the relevant lymphocytes are taken from patients before their immune defence systems, already in a less than perfect state, are further compromised by the kind of drugs used to treat the diseases concerned. They are then stored at very low temperatures, and thawed out again after the treatment has been carried out, in order to restore as high a level of immune defence function as possible.

At the time of writing, research is being carried out into the successful cloning of the T and B cells of animals. These cloned cells can be prepared in such a way that they are geared to fight a particular disease. The appropriately cloned cells are reinjected into the donor animal when required. Here, they augment its natural defence mechanisms, thereby increasing its resistance to cancer, infections and other disease-provoking agents.

The future prospects for cell therapy include storing young T cells at very low temperatures where they remain alive and in a healthy condition, to be used later to increase lifespan. Another means of boosting the immune system which is still being investigated at laboratory level is with nucleic acid injections. Mice given yeast nucleic acids responded with a sixteen per cent lifespan prolongation. Professor Walford has speculated that we may be able to devise means of augmenting our own DNA repair processes by means of 'property altered' DNA injections.

HELPING YOURSELF

We have reviewed, in this chapter, much that is currently known and much that is currently being investigated about boosting the vitality of the immune defence system by taking supplements in addition to a low-calorie, high-nutrition diet. The most desirable practical outcome is that you know what to take, and when to take it, in order to invigorate your own immune defences. A practicable system of immune defence supplementation has been worked out, and I am going to provide it here.

Recently, a special food-supplement formula was developed with a view to reinforcing the immune defence system against the possibility of contracting AIDS, or, for that matter, any other infection. It is quite impossible – and it would be totally unethical – to guarantee results, and all that can be said for this, or any other, dietary supplement, aimed at producing a particular effect, is that it offers the best help possible at a nutritional level bearing in mind our current state of knowledge on the subject.

The formula[9] contains many of the major nutrients known to be involved in immune functions, including a number of important free amino acids, vitamins and minerals. Not all the amino acids have been mentioned in this chapter, simply because space has not permitted. In addition to the formula presented here, it is recommended by the manufacturers that certain other supplements be taken in addition (ie, evening primrose oil, beta carotene – the precursor of vitamin A, vitamin A as such, together with vitamin D, and extra vitamin C). I have myself added one or two extras at the end, starred thus*.

9. *Nutrition News* (no. 104), Felmore Ltd (Health Publications), 1 Lamberts Road, PO Box 1, Tunbridge Wells TN2 3EQ, UK

ESSENTIAL SUPPLEMENTS CHART TO MAXIMISE YOUR HEALTH AND VITALITY____

L-Arginine	140mg	Vitamin B1	20mg
L-Ornithine	40mg	Vitamin B2	20mg
Glycine	40mg	Vitamin B6	32mg
L-Taurine	40mg	Vitamin B12	200mcg
L-Cystine	40mg	Vitamin C	40mg
L-Glutamic Acid	20mg	Pantothenic Acid	32mg
L-Alanine	20mg	Folic Acid	80mcg
L-Tyrosine	20mg	Sorbitol	8mg
L-Tryptophane	20mg	Magnesium Amino Chelate	40mg
L-Histidine	20mg	Selenium as	
L-Methionine	20mg	Seleno-methionine	20mcg
L-Lysine	20mg	Zinc as gluconate	3.2mg

In addition, the following should be taken:

Evening primrose oil (Efamol)	500mg, three times daily
Beta carotene	15mg, once or twice daily with meals
Vitamin A, with	7,500IU
Vitamin D	400IU, one capsule daily of each with a meal
Vitamin C, in either powder or tablet form	As much as the bowel will tolerate, 3 or 4 times daily
Vitamin E*	600IU daily
BHT*	150mg daily
Raw thymus gland	
Interferon	All according to maker's instructions
Co-enzyme Q	

In cases of special need, triple the daily intake of the formulated capsules to a daily intake of five capsules three times daily, half an hour before each meal.

7 How Fresh Air and Exercise Aid Resistance to Infection

The idea that fresh air is essential to health is probably as old as the human race. Cave man, sitting round a smoky fire which made him cough and his eyes smart, must often have wandered off from the mouth of his cave in search of the cooling night breeze. Hut dwellers, whose only source of warmth was a log or peat fire located in the centre of the un-chimneyed habitation, doubtless choked, spat and gasped for fresh, clean air as the stench of unwashed bodies, wood smoke and roasting meat assailed their senses.

Even nomadic tribes, exposed for far longer periods of time to wind and weather, avoided areas of encampment located too close to stinking bogs, pit traps of rotting animal bones, and bad smelling marshland. Right up to the Middle Ages and beyond, conditions of hygiene and ventilation were not a great deal better. Of course most people, even the poorest, lived in houses equipped with the basic amenities. Windows let in light and air, doors did likewise, and chimneys were constructed in such a way that at least some of the smoke went out of the house at roof level. Yet the sawdust floors collected food and cooking debris, farm and domestic animals dwelt in close proximity to their owners, and arrangements for sanitation and the disposal of waste were, to put it mildly, extremely basic. Chamberpots, for instance, were simply emptied when necessary into the gutters outside, already overflowing with garbage, rotting vegetation, rainwater and street mud. The importance of frequent baths, with plenty of hot water and soap, was as yet undreamed of. Even Elizabeth I was said to hate washing, and to keep the same undergarments on without changing them, for months at a time.

It is little wonder, when you come to consider the matter, that nosegays of sweet-smelling flowers sold so well at street corners, or that dried oranges stuck with cloves were popular additions to ladies' wardrobes. It is equally easy to see why the making of lavender bags, pot-pourris and pomanders came to number among our national country crafts, and why gentlemen were as perfumed and powdered when they appeared in public as were their ladyfolk.

There were two reasons why bad smells were disguised whenever possible, why stuffy, overheated rooms were considered unhealthy, and why country air and sea breezes were sought by sick people in a position to pay for what they wanted. For one thing, offensive odours do quite simply 'offend' and make people attempt to remove themselves forthwith. For another, stale air was associated in most peoples' minds with sickness and disease.

It is essential to remember that, prior to the nineteenth century, nothing was known about the nature of infectious illnesses nor about how they were transmitted. Poverty inevitably involved overcrowding, malnutrition, filthy living conditions, and a high mortality rate – frequently from diseases that could be seen to spread like wildfire. Bad odours, extremes of temperature depending upon the prevailing weather conditions, and poor ventilation were quite logically indicated as at least in part responsible.

We only have to think of John Snow, mentioned in an earlier chapter as having traced the source of a cholera outbreak to a contaminated water supply, to be reminded that the consensus of contemporary medical opinion attributed the sickness instead to noxious vapours in the air. The notion that poor-quality air actually *caused* infectious illnesses was quite erroneous. All the same, the superstitious belief contained at least a grain of truth.

Bad smells in the air do not cause infectious illnesses. They are simply a by-product of the prevailing conditions that inevitably foster the rapid transmission of bacterial and viral diseases. Frequently associated with overcrowding and poor ventilation, however, are a build-up of the waste product carbon dioxide, and a relative shortage of our bodies' most vital ingredient – oxygen. This is the point at which the old superstitions regarding the origins of disease, and up to date knowledge of physiology and biochemistry, find their meeting point.

THE ROLE OF OXYGEN

Oxygen is vital to all the living tissues of the body. The more vital the organ, the greater its need for an uninterrupted supply of this essential element. You have only to consider the heart and the brain, to realise the dire effects of cutting off a person's oxygen source.

When someone is unfortunate enough to suffer a cardiac arrest (ie, cessation of the heart's pumping action, and therefore a pause in the activity of the circulatory system), three minutes only are available to would-be helpers if they are to restore the patient to life and health. External cardiac massage must be started immediately, and air must be introduced into and out of the patient's lungs by mouth-to-mouth resuscitation. If these actions are not started soon enough, or are carried out inefficiently, the vulnerable cells of the brain and heart suffer irrevocable damage.

The agonising pain of a coronary is due to an acute oxygen shortage in the heart muscle, just as a stroke results from the cutting off of the blood (and therefore the oxygen) supply to an area of brain. If small areas of heart muscle and brain tissue are thus deprived of vital oxygen, the patient recovers, and gradually regains full functional capacity. If an extensive area of either organ is oxygen starved, then the heart attack or stroke can be fatal.

To a less dramatic, but equally serious extent in the long run, all the tissues of the body suffer when they receive insufficient oxygen. The state of mesotrophy, mentioned earlier in connection with the naturopathic view of disease and health, is very frequently associated with an inadequate supply of tissue oxygen. A variety of causes exist for this state of affairs, including diseased arteries, a malfunctioning heart, and a number of metabolic defects. One of the commonest, however, is inadequate oxygenation of the lungs due to a sedentary lifestyle!

The reason why oxygen is so vital is that it is the sole means the body possesses of providing itself with a supply of energy from the food it takes in for the purpose. Energy is required for every one of the thousands of metabolic activities that take place in our brain, muscle, nerve, cardiac and blood cells, every moment we are alive.

Digested food is useless unless molecules of oxygen are provided by the blood supply to any given area. The chemical equation representing the 'burning' of food, the consequent release of energy, and the excretion of water and carbon dioxide as waste products, simply cannot take place. Here is what happens under normal conditions.

THE CIRCULATION OF THE BLOOD_____

The heart is divided into four chambers, an upper right chamber (atrium) which communicates with the lower right ventricle below it, and an upper left atrium, separate from the right, but communicating, like the right, with a left chamber or ventricle immediately below it. The two sides of the heart are completely separate and only in abnormal conditions, such as 'hole in the heart' does a communication exist between the chambers on the right and those on the left.

Blood is returned by large veins from the tissues, into the right atrium. In this condition, the blood contains all the metabolic waste materials it has picked up as it traversed the body, and possesses very little oxygen. Because of this, it has a bluish colour. Only arterial blood, that has recently picked up a supply of oxygen from the lungs, is bright red.

From the right atrium, the blood is squeezed through one-way valves into the right ventricle, which in turn pumps it through the pulmonary artery and into the lungs. As it circulates through the lung tissues, the blood travels through extremely thin vessels, and comes into sufficiently close contact with the air within the lungs' cavities for oxygen to filter through to it.

As this happens, the oxygen-transport pigment within the red blood cells (ie, haemoglobin) 'picks up' the gaseous oxygen and attaches itself to it chemically. Simultaneously, the carbon dioxide present in the blood, leaves the circulation and passes out into the lungs' air sacs. It is expelled into the atmosphere when the next breath is exhaled, and a further fresh oxygen supply is obtained when the next breath is drawn.

The oxygen-rich blood then leaves the lungs via the pulmonary veins, which enter the left atrium chamber of the heart. From here, it passes into the left ventricle and thence into the aorta, the body's largest artery. This leaves the left side of the heart and passes down through the chest and abdomen, sending off small arterial branches to all the main organs and tissues. It finally culminates in the pelvis in the pair of iliac arteries, which supply the lower limbs with arterial (ie, oxygenated) blood.

When arterial blood enters the body's tissues or an organ, it travels through smaller and smaller blood vessels (arterioles) until it finally enters the smallest vessels of all, the capillaries. These have extremely thin walls, consisting of a single layer of cells only, and it is between the blood within these vessels and the surrounding tissues that the vital gaseous exchange takes place.

Oxygen passes outwards, together with the nutrients the cells require, while the oxygen-hungry cells relinquish their waste products, including carbon dioxide. These are transported from the area, first in capillaries, then in the slightly larger venules (tiny veins), then in the veins themselves which eventually return the de-oxygenated blood to the right atrium. From there it re-enters the lungs, and the circulatory process repeats itself.

WHY YOU NEED EXERCISE

As we mentioned in Chapter 2, mesotrophy (the undesirable state of health in which we are especially prone to contract diseases) comes about largely because metabolic wastes are allowed to accumulate in the tissues. When mesotrophy is present, the immune defence system is essentially weakened, and we are more than usually susceptible to the effects of invading enemies. These include the long-term problem factors such as environmental toxins and the effects of radiation, as well as the shorter term, more immediate factors such as pathogenic bacteria and viruses.

Mesotrophy, therefore, is clearly to be avoided at all costs, if we wish to remain in optimal health and free from infectious illnesses. It is, however, the state most of us are in, if we eat junk food and/or fail to exercise sufficiently. Exercise is not just a health gimmick, conjured up by the wealthy owners of gymnasia and health spars, and the editors of health and fitness magazines, to make us lesser mortals feel a unique combination of irritation, envy and guilt. Exercise *actually matters* very much if you really do want to remain infection free.

Daily exercise is one of the best possible ways of maintaining and retaining a healthy circulatory system. Selecting the variety that makes the right sort of demand on the heart – never too much, and never too little – is the best possible way of ensuring that the circulatory systems stay in optimal functioning order. This means that waste products are given no opportunity to accumulate in the tissue spaces, and that we have an excellent chance of reverting from the mesotrophic condition to one of abundant health and vitality.

In this way, our immune defence systems are given maximum chance to function effectively, and we have the best possible hope not only of remaining well, but also of retarding the ageing process and hopefully avoiding cancer and degenerative disease.

The truth is that diet alone, even extensively supplemented as described in the last chapter, is not enough in itself to ensure the health of the immune defences. We have to make an extra effort. We have actually to get out there – every day – and challenge our hearts, arteries and circulatory systems to give of their very best. This is one of the finest and one of the surest methods available for staying both as young and as disease free as possible.

Besides avoiding the accumulation of tissue waste, and making us far more disease resistant, regular exercise has further benefits. The rejuvenatory effects of exercise are due, not only to the positive effects upon the immune defences, but also to the direct effects upon heart muscle, artery and blood pressure. It is practically impossible to be overweight if you eat sensibly and exercise regularly, and obesity is a major factor in the generation of hypertension, atheromatous (ie, furred-up) arteries and coronary thromboses.

In addition, therapeutic exercise lowers the blood levels of LDLPs (low-density lipoproteins) and cholesterol, both known to play key roles in the deposition of atheromatous arterial lesions. It helps to guard against loss of calcium from the bones, a fact of major importance to everybody, especially women at the time of the menopause. It speeds up the metabolic rate, which results in the optimum use of food fuel energy, and ensures that oxygen supplied to the tissues is utilised as efficiently as possible.

A further relevant fact about the benefits of exercise, when we are considering resistance to infections and environmental toxins, is that a healthy circulatory system does wonders for our first-line defence mechanisms A sluggish blood flow, and the deposition of toxic waste in the tissues, make for weakened mucous membranes and unhealthy skin. These, in turn, affect the efficiency with which we deal with invading bacteria and viruses, the condition of our first-line defences in the mouth cavity, respiratory tract, stomach, bowel and genito-urinary tract, and whether useful bacteria can continue to flourish where they are most needed.

Efficient arterial supply of well-oxygenated blood to a body area maintains the healthy condition of its constituent cells, just as adequate and prompt venous drainage removes metabolic waste material before it has the opportunity to collect.

Aerobic exercise

There are many approaches to exercise. The type you choose, depends upon what you are setting out to accomplish. Yoga, T'ai Chi and therapeutic dance are all valuable forms of therapy, and offer litheness and flexibility, and a greater capacity to deal with stress.

Exercise designed to improve the functional ability of the heart, circulation and lungs, however, has to be 'aerobic', that is, it has to increase the need of the body's tissues for supplies of oxygen and fuel. You can tell when exercise is aerobic, by the fact that your pulse rate increases and your lungs demand a greater supply of air. Puffing and panting to some degree are an inevitable part of aerobic activity, especially at first when you have not exercised for a considerable time. However, by observing your pulse rate carefully, you can make certain not to overtax your heart or lung reserve.

There are many excellent books written about exercise. Space does not allow us to go into great detail here, but the importance of pulse rates in relation to exercise must be stressed. Moreover, it is well worth pointing out the necessity of choosing a type of exercise that appeals to you! There is absolutely no need to martyr yourself in the cause of good health, and no value at all in choosing something to do on a regular basis that you do not enjoy! This almost inevitably results in the loathed activity being abandoned after only a few days of effort, with no conceivable benefit to anyone.

Pulse rates Once you have selected tap dancing, jogging, swimming, cycling or an aerobic class where lots of different exercises are performed to music, make certain that you monitor your pulse rate every time you exercise. The maximum heart rate advisable for you to reach, is calculated by subtracting your age from 220. To gain the benefits of aerobic training, you should exercise your heart at sixty per cent of this rate if you are unfit, or eighty per cent if fit. You should refer to Table 2 in order to find your correct training rate.

If you are between the ages given, refer to the higher age rather than the lower, that is, if you are forty one, refer to age forty-five on the Table rather than to forty. Take your pulse by placing the tips of your index and middle fingers of one hand on the inside of the wrist of the other hand. Count the beats for half a minute and multiply by two. Your resting pulse rate indicates your present state of fitness, provided that you are not taking any drugs or food substances capable of accelerating the rate of the heart beat. Examples are certain antidepressant drugs, caffeine, and of course tea and coffee containing caffeine. Fear and excitement also speed the pulse up, due to the release of adrenalin. The best time to take your resting pulse rate, therefore, is first thing in the morning after you wake up, and before you have anything to eat or drink. Consult Table 1 to find out how fit you are.

Table 1*   Resting Pulse Rate Fitness Guide

Beats per minute

Under 60	— very fit	80 – 90	— below average
60 – 70	— fit		
70 – 80	— average	Over 90	— unfit

It is also important to check how quickly your heart recovers from exercise. Take your pulse five minutes after stopping. It should not exceed 120 beats per minute, and if it does, then you have exercised too vigorously. As you get fitter, your recovery rate will improve, but you will also have to work harder to reach your recommended training rate. Build up your stamina gradually – do not simply exercise more rapidly, as this may make you exceed your training rate and annul the benefits from the workout.

How long you exercise for is very important. Minimum workout times appear in the chart below. Once you are starting to feel fitter, exercise for at least twenty minutes, preferably thirty to forty

*Courtesy of *Living* magazine

Table 2							
Age Years	Max. Heart Rate	Exercise Rate if Fit Beats per minute	Exercise Rate if Unfit Beats per minute	Age Years	Max. Heart Rate	Exercise Rate if Fit Beats per minute	Exercise Rate if Unfit Beats per minute
16	204	164	133	34	186	149	121
18	202	162	132	36	184	148	120
20	200	160	130	38	182	146	119
22	198	158	129	40	180	144	117
24	196	157	128	45	175	140	114
26	194	155	127	50	170	136	111
28	192	154	125	55	165	132	108
30	190	152	124	60	160	128	104
32	188	151	123	65	155	124	101

Time Chart: *Minimum Workout Times**

12 minutes	15 minutes	20 minutes
Running on the spot	Jogging	Brisk walking
Skipping	Distance running	Cycling
Trampolining	Rowing	Skating
Competitive swimming	Dancing	Swimming

minutes, at least four times weekly. If you have not exercised for a very long time, start by walking. Walk at first at your normal pace, and then halfway through the walk, speed up to a faster pace for five minutes, then slow down again to your normal pace. Always check your pulse at the end of the first five minutes and also five minutes later. As you get fitter you can increase five minutes to ten and so on.

Alternatively, you can do two spurts each lasting three minutes on your walk. Just find the method that suits you best, and stick to it. In addition, remember to start all exercise with gentle warming up exercises, jogging slowly on the spot, flexing arms and legs, touching your toes and so on. End exercise bouts with similar slowing down actions, too.

If you suffer from any illness or are recovering from one, especially high blood pressure, angina, or other circulatory problems, *always* have a medical check-up first, and consult your doctor before commencing any exercise routine.

*(Courtesy of *Living* magazine)

Deep breathing exercises   The value of controlled breathing has been recognised for many centuries. Breath control is an essential aspect both of Chinese medicine and of yoga, and it will be mentioned again in the latter context in the next chapter, when we consider various means of learning to relax.

Some of the benefits of deep breathing include better oxygenation of the blood, a greater feeling of calmness, improved sleep, and increased resistance to diseases, especially infectious ones. You have only to think of the inner passages of the nose, throat, voice box (larynx), wind-pipe (trachea) and lungs, with their delicate membranous linings and their continual subjection to all the debris, dust, bacteria, viruses, airborne toxins and pollutants. The less 'well aired' the respiratory tract area, the greater the chance of this first line of defence failing to do its job, and the greater the chance for pathogens to breed in the stagnant mucus.

Taking lungfuls of fresh air (always try to exercise out of doors, by the way, or at least close to an open window) washes out much of the collecting noxious material with a current of fresh, well-oxygenated air which is generally at a lower temperature than that of the enclosed air spaces. Pathogens characteristically like dark, warm, moist areas in which to breed and some of them have a strong dislike of oxygen in any form.

It is easy to see why, say, a dozen breaths of the cleanest outdoor air you can find, taken *slowly* in to full lung capacity, held for as long as is comfortable, and expired slowly, at least three times daily, can decrease the number of infections to which you fall prey.

AIR IONISERS

So great is many peoples' belief in the curative powers of fresh air, that cans of 'mountain air' found a ready market some years ago, among people desperate enough about their health to 'try anything once'. Nevertheless, although I believe this to have been a 'catchpenny' aimed at removing money from the pockets of gullible people, mountain air is a great deal healthier than what many of us breathe in offices, factories, city streets, and even our homes.

Ordinary uncontaminated air consists of a mixture of gases, the chief constituents of which are nitrogen (about eighty per cent) and oxygen (in the region of twenty per cent); the remainder consisting of carbon dioxide, water vapour, and what are known as the 'rare gases', argon, xenon, krypton. These various gases are present in the form of gaseous molecules, which under ordinary conditions are electrically neutral (neither positively nor negatively charged)[10].

Pure mountain air, for instance, contains only about 4,000 charged ions in every two million, million, million. If ions are unbalanced, then they become harmful, especially when they bear positive charges. Many people are adversely affected by air bearing a positive charge. They are the ones who become sensitive to a change in the atmosphere of 'thunder in the air'. Positively charged air ions have been found to predominate in buildings with central heating systems, of which many people complain. Conversely, many others feel very much below par in towns where there is a good deal of dust, toxic fumes and smoke in the atmosphere.

Air ionisers are machines which artificially produce negatively charged air particles or ions. These have been found to benefit people in terms not only of subjective well-being, but also in terms of their work output and performance. In a trial conducted in England by the department of Human Biology and Health at the University of Surrey, the work performance of forty-five volunteers was examined when they were subjected to a positively charged atmosphere, a normal atmosphere and a negatively charged one.

The performances of the volunteers rose in the morning and the afternoon, and declined in the evening, when working in a normal atmosphere. The same thing happened when they were in a positively charged atmosphere, except that their declining performance was more noticeable. Those in a negatively charged atmosphere maintained a high performance level all day.

In the 1970s, Professor A. P. Kreuger's work at the University of California showed that negatively charged ions can be used to destroy harmful bacteria. There is very probably a great deal more to the explanation of air ionisation's benefits, but it is used as a form of therapy for people suffering from respiratory tract problems, including sinusitis, hay fever, asthma, and chronic catarrh. The treatment seems to be especially effective when administered regularly on an overnight basis. Atmospheric ionisation also creates a sense of well-being in people who are normally subjected to air

10. Inglis, B. and West, R. *The Alternative Health Guide* Michael Joseph, London, pages 38–9

pollution, atmospheric dust and conditions generally shown to create positive ionisation.

Using an air ioniser when working, in addition to eating a whole food, supplemented diet and exercising regularly, could pay dividends in terms of your increased resistance to infections.

SKIN BRUSHING

While it is tempting to say plenty on the topic of exercising for a healthier blood circulatory system, it is important not to forget the well-being of the lymphatic drainage system which plays such an important part in removing toxic debris and waste material, and helping to protect us from a state of mesotrophy.

Skin brushing is a technique for encouraging the elimination of wastes through the skin, and stimulating lymphatic drainage. Leslie and Susannah Kenton are experts on this topic, which they introduced in their best-selling book *Raw Energy* (Century Publishing). They advocate it as a tried and tested way of getting rid of cellulite, when combined with an aerobic exercise programme and a diet based on raw vegetables and fruits, nuts, seeds and sprouts.

Leslie and Susannah suggest that the best way is to use a long-handled natural bristle brush or a hemp glove. Both your skin and the brush or glove should be dry. Brush your entire body area, except for your face, starting at the soles of your feet, then moving upwards with firm, sweeping movements. Brush your front gently, using clockwise, circular brush strokes over the area of your abdomen. Take a warm shower afterwards, followed by a cold one for thirty seconds only. Dry yourself and keep warm. The two authors point out that:

Because of its stimulating action on the tissues beneath the skin, regular skin brushing encourages efficient lymphatic drainage. It is an extra-ordinarily efficient technique for cleansing the lymphatic system and for clearing away waste materials from the cells all over the body as well as those – as in the case of cellulite – that have become trapped between the cells where they are held by hardened connective tissue and where they build up to create pockets of water, toxins and fat that give the skin its *peau d'orange* (orange skin) appearance.

8 The Importance of Sleep and Relaxation

The state of sleep has been celebrated, and the lack of it bemoaned, by poets throughout the ages. Coleridge says feelingly of it in his 'Ancient Mariner': 'Oh sleep! it is a gentle thing,/Beloved from pole to pole'. The seventeenth-century poet, Edward Young, calls it: 'Tired Nature's sweet restorer, balmy sleep'.

Shakespeare's satanic Iago, delighted that his lies about Desdemona's virtue are ruining Othello's tranquillity of mind, says 'Nor poppy, nor mandragora,/Nor all the drowsy syrups of the world,/Shall ever medicine thee to that sweet sleep/Which thou owedst yesterday'.

Perhaps the most pertinent of all, in the context of this chapter, are Macbeth's words following his murder of Duncan, in which he refers to the sleep (not only Duncan's, but his own and others') that he has destroyed: '. . . sleep that knits up the ravelled sleeve of care . . . Balm of hurt minds, great nature's second course,/Chief nourisher in life's feast'.

Sleep is all these things and, more scientifically, many others as well. It is, however, something that we tend not to think a great deal about unless we are either not getting enough of it, or conversely are plagued by continual drowsiness. Sleep disorders are a common problem in our society. Of greatest relevance to the immune defence system is the fact that tissue repair processes take place most effectively during the hours of repose. Good quality sleep is also essential to counteract stress.

SLEEP AND REPAIR PROCESSES

It is very common for 'rest', either bedrest or a rest from normal activities, to be prescribed during and following an illness. The purpose of this is not only to enable the invalid to bear with his symptoms the better, but also to give the body's recuperative powers maximum opportunity to work. They are most likely to function when little else is going on in the body, simply because far more of the body's energy and strength are available for the purpose.

If rest from exertion, a light diet, and freedom from stress are all part of the acknowledged treatment of disease, they are as an extension of this, just as vital to the round-the-clock repair processes that our bodies carry out. They are necessary throughout our lives, regardless of whether on the surface we remain disease and injury free.

The outer surface of the skin's epidermal layer is being perpetually shed, and renewed from below (see Chapter 3). The surface mucosal cells lining the intestines, genital tract and other organs, are being continually replaced. Hair and nails grow long, are trimmed, and replenish themselves from living tissue below. And throughout the body, blood cells, platelets and blood proteins are being manufactured, antibodies are being called into play or new ones fashioned to cope with strange invaders. Bone, muscle, connective tissue, blood vessels and lymphatic tissue also maintain a constant need for replenishment.

Sleep clearly affords the best opportunity for the diversion of the body's energy and rebuilding powers towards these essential activities. The amount of sleep we as individuals require, differs according to age, as does the pattern of sleep cycles. By these, are meant the relative amounts of the two different varieties of sleep that have been identified, nonrapid eye movement sleep (NREM) and rapid eye movement sleep (REM).

It is worth considering these two briefly, as knowing a little about them is essential if the biochemistry of sleep in terms of neurotransmitter function is to be explained even in the simplest terms. The reason, in turn, why this is pertinent to our discussion, is that regular sleep of the right quality is essential to health in general, and our immune defences in particular. A natural dietary supplement working in close association with brain neurotransmitter biochemistry is available to help restore normal sleeping patterns in people who suffer from insomnia.

WHAT HAPPENS WHEN YOU SLEEP

Every night's sleep consists of a series of biphasic 90 to 100 minute cycles, in which the two different phases of sleep both occur. The NREM phase (also known as slow-wave or synchronised sleep) is the one you enter as you doze off, and this type also initiates each subsequent cycle. If an EEG (electro-encephalogram) tracing is taken, brain waves are seen to slow during NREM phases, and other physiological tests have shown that there is a corresponding decrease in muscle tone, heart rate, respiratory rate and blood pressure.

If you are roused mid-cycle, when NREM is at its height, then you appear (and feel!) disorientated, confused and very much as though you have been 'woken at the wrong time'! The REM sleep phase, which follows NREM and ends each cycle, is also known as fast-wave or desynchronised sleep. The brain waves can be seen on an EEG tracing to become more active, and heart rate, blood pressure and respiratory rate to rise correspondingly as well.

Paradoxically, though, muscle tone is even more relaxed in REM sleep than it is in NREM. An exception to this, is the muscles that move the eyes within their sockets. During this sleep phase, the eyes have been described as 'executing spectacular runs of nystagmiform [ie, jerky] movement behind the still-closed lids'. When you wake from REM sleep, you are readily roused, far better orientated, and may well be able to give a vivid account of your dreams.

This NREM-REM cycle repeats itself, usually without interruption, four or five times each night. During later cycles (towards the morning) relatively more sleep time is devoted to REM. Research into the biochemical mechanism of sleep has revealed that the control centre of the alternating sleep phases and cycle is located in the brain stem (the lower part of the brain, where it tapers downwards and becomes continuous with the spinal cord).

Neurotransmitters and control of circadian rhythm

It seems that two interconnected groups of neurones (brain cells) counterbalance and oppose one another's actions. One group, known as adrenergic because their neurotransmitters (chemical messengers) are adrenalin and noradrenalin, has predominant effect during REM sleep. The other, known as cholinergic because their neurotransmitter is acetylcholine, holds sway during NREM sleep. Their alternating (phasic) activity is due to the push-pull (reciprocal) interaction of the excitatory (adrenergic) and inhibitory (cholinergic) neurotransmitters that mediate their activities.

Our tendency to be wakeful during daylight hours, and increasingly sleepy at night, is a familiar example of the fact that the metabolism of all organisms is temporally ordered. Cosmic forces synchronise circadian rhythms – the inborn biological cycles of just under twenty-five hours in length which are reset each day by light as well as other time cues. In all mammals, including man, the control headquarters of repeated circadian cycles seems to be located in the hypothalmic area of the midbrain.

This receives a direct input from the optic nerves which pick up light stimuli, and it is thought that these light pulsations reset the body's rhythms each day. If you have crossed time zones in a jet aircraft, you will know how powerful and persistent the circadian control of your sleeping and waking needs can be.

We can be sure, however, that chemical neurotransmitters (adrenaline, noradrenaline, acetycholine) play a vital role in alternating the two different types of sleep, and that they may well be the means by which circadian sleep patterns are mediated and controlled. The adrenergic (REM-controlling) neurones referred to above, can be identified as mainly 'waking' cells – they are more active than their opponents (the 'sleeping' cholinergic neurones) during waking periods. The brain nuclei (concentrated clumps of nerve tissue) containing the 'waking' cells, are believed to control three major functions – the sleeping state, mood and learning.

Natural insomnia remedies

Tryptophan   This is one of the essential amino acids we mentioned earlier in this book. Apart from its being essential in the synthesis of nicotinic acid (one of the B complex vitamins), tryptophan has been used therapeutically in the treatment of both insomnia and depression. Like all other potent chemical agents, this amino acid must be used with care. One cannot safely say that because any substance is naturally occurring, then it is perfectly safe to take under any circumstances and in whatever quantities one likes.

Tryptophan should be taken in the doses recommended here or by a qualified nutritional therapist only. Also, it is not recommended for pregnant women, or for women trying to conceive, and it is incompatible (meaning that it should *never* be taken in conjunction) with MAOI antidepressant drugs (the monamine oxidase inhibitors), eg, tranylcypromine; isocarboxazid phenelzine. It should also be avoided by anyone who is taking levo-dopa, the anti-Parkinsonian drug, and anyone with an active disease of the bladder.

Having mentioned the precautions, it is also fair to say that tryptophan has acquired a well-deserved reputation for itself as a potent sleep-inducing agent and antidepressant. Both effects are likely to occur in anyone taking it, but we are concentrating here upon its safe sleep-inducing properties. If you need to sleep better but do not suffer from depression, that is no contraindication to your taking it. It will only elevate the mood to a 'normal' level; it will lighten the mood of a depressed person, but will not make a non-depressed poor sleeper 'high' and euphoric.

Tryptophan is a nutrient affecting neurotransmitter function[11]. It is converted by enzyme action into 5-HT (5-hydroxytryptamine), and this in turn is converted into serotonin, a neurotransmitter. It works as a sleep-inducer, because serotonin stimulates the cholinergic ('sleeping') neurones we discussed above. Tryptophan was investigated as serotonin's precursor in this context by Dr E. Hartmann of Boston State Hospital. He reported:

In our studies, we found that a dose of one gram of tryptophan will cut down the time it takes to fall asleep from twenty to ten minutes. Its great advantage is that not only do you get to sleep sooner, but you do so without distortions in sleep patterns that are produced by most sleeping pills[11].

Researchers Goldberg and Kauffman state that they replicated Hartmann's results and found that tryptophan did not in any way

11. Chaitow, L. *Amino Acids in Therapy* Thorsons Publishers, Wellingborough, UK, pages 63–9

depress the central nervous system but 'simply allowed the body to do what it normally does under ideal conditions'[11].

A summary of the effects of tryptophan on sleep was given in a study in California[11]. Firstly it was found that tryptophan was an effective hypnotic (sleep inducer) when administered at any time of day. Further, it was found to reduce significantly the time of sleep onset without affecting the various stages of sleep. Finally it was shown that tryptophan produces a more relaxed waking state forty-five minutes after ingestion, and that at this stage sleep may be induced if required.

By combining vitamin B6 (pyridoxine) and magnesium with tryptophan the effects of tryptophan just described were enhanced. Vitamin C has also been found to enhance the uptake of tryptophan by the brain, when pyridoxine was given at the same time.

A massive amount of research has been carried out into the mechanisms whereby brain function is altered in relation to serum levels of the dietary nutrients influencing neurotransmitter production. Besides tryptophan, these include the amino acid tyrosine (which is ultimately converted into adrenalin); and lecithin in its pure form phosphatidylcholine, which becomes the neurotransmitter choline.

It has been revealed that serum levels of serotonin influence the individual's choice of food, so that more or less carbohydrate will be consumed. Wurtmann, who has researched this area exhaustively, has found that by altering amounts of carbohydrate eaten it is possible to increase the levels of serotonin in the brain. Tryptophan brain levels, ready for conversion into serotonin, depend upon serum tryptophan levels as well as the ratio between plasma tryptophan and five other amino acids (tyrosine, phenylalanine, leucine, isoleucine, and valine).

Since a high-protein meal leaves much less tryptophan free for the passage across the membrane known as the blood-brain barrier, and thence into the brain itself, than other amino acids, less tryptophan actually enters the brain. In other words, a meal containing tryptophan but high in other amino acids, reduces rather than increases the amount of tryptophan in the brain. A high-carbohydrate meal, on the other hand, induces insulin release, and this has a marked effect upon the five amino acids just mentioned

11. Chaitow, L. *Amino Acids in Therapy* Thorsons Publishers, Wellingborough, UK, pages 63–9

because they are circulating as free molecules, which tryptophan is not.

Therefore, tryptophan can enter the brain with far more ease, and a small carbohydrate snack is advised to be taken with tryptophan when used as a sleep supplement. It is interesting to note that the old 'home remedy' of a glass of hot milk on retiring, as a good means of getting to sleep, has (as so often proves the case) some valid scientific foundation. Milk neutralises stomach acid, and also contains both tryptophan and the carbohydrate lactose, or milk sugar. It is an ideal natural substance to help induce drowsiness last thing at night, especially when taken together with a tryptophan supplement. (The other tryptophan enhancers, vitamins C and B6, and magnesium, are also supplied by the daily vitamin and mineral complex already discussed in the chapter on dietary supplements).

Tryptophan is also prescribable as a drug on the British National Health Service for depression (although many doctors now also prescribe it for sleeplessness). The recommended dose is two tablets three times a day, each tablet containing 500mg of 1-tryptophan (the 1-refers to a particular molecular configuration of tryptophan, this being the one you should take!), in combination with 10mg of ascorbic acid (a form of vitamin C), and 5mg pyridoxine.

Health nutritionists vary in the amount of tryptophan they advise for the treatment of poor sleep without depression. 1g nightly seems to be adequate for most people. Some researchers have found that as much as 5g are needed to tackle insomnia effectively. Individuals differ a great deal in their response to both drugs and dietary nutrients and supplements, and no results can ever be guaranteed. All the same, my own recommendation would be to try a gram of tryptophan at night and if you feel it is partly successful but that you may require more of it, consult your doctor or a nutritional expert.

Inositol This has already been mentioned in the chapter dealing with vitamins as a (water-soluble) member of the B complex. Its effect upon the quantitative brain waves of both patients and normal volunteers has been extensively studied at the Brain Bio Center in Princeton, New Jersey by the well-known research scientist Dr Carl Pfeiffer and co-workers. It has been shown to have a typical antianxiety effect similar to that of chlordiazepoxide (Librium) or meprobamate (Equanil)[12]. It also has sedative properties, and, says Dr Pfeiffer, 'solves many insomnia and anxiety problems'. In animals, the nutrients that work closely with inositol include pantothenic acid, pyridoxine, folic acid, choline, methionine, and betaine, which (like choline, methionine and inositol itself) is a lipotropic substance. This refers to the function of preventing abnormal or excessive accumulations of fat in the cells of the liver.

Inositol is available in 250 and 500mg tablets from various suppliers. Their dose directions should be followed if you are taking this vitamin alone as an additional supplement, rather than (or in addition to) the inositol already being provided by your daily multivitamin supplement.

RELAXATION

Most people think they know how to relax. When asked to describe how they go about it, they relate their habits of television watching, reading or making love. In actual fact, none of these pastimes in themselves is especially conducive to relaxation even in the broadest sense. Many television addicts sit curled up in an armchair, tensely anticipating the next projected move of the characters in 'Dallas'.

Many avid readers pore over the latest crime novel or historical fiction, lying in bed with the electric blanket on far too high a setting and their neck muscles tense because of the 'comfortable' posture they are involuntarily adopting. Lovemaking may also count in your book as a pleasurable activity, as well it should. However, few people relax during it, although the rest that follows a satisfactory orgasm is among the most profound known. What can be said with certainty is that it is almost impossible to relax your muscles, nerves and mind while actually 'on the job'.

Foreplay to the satisfying sexual act actually demands a fair amount of physical exertion, and coitus itself (to give it its scientific name) can burn up a fair number of calories.

True relaxation demands total 'give' on behalf of body, mind and soul. Paradoxically, it is difficult to achieve, and the harder you try to relax, the more difficult it becomes. The moment you cease to try,

12. Pfeiffer, C. *Mental and Elemental Nutrients* Keats Publishing, Inc, Connecticut, USA, page 145

and simply 'flow' with the waves of the life force in your immediate vicinity, then you will discover what true relaxation really means.

To know what it feels like to be *really* relaxed, you have to think what you feel like when you wake up in the morning, at the stage when you are only just 'coming to' and have not yet begun to wonder whether the alarm has already gone off, whether it is Saturday or Wednesday, or whether you have a dental appointment that day. In other words, you feel warm, comfortable and utterly 'giving', your thoughts are drifting pleasantly through your conscious mind at a very ponderous rate, and you are aware of normally 'subliminal' stimuli such as the pleasing coolness of the sheet beneath you, and the gentle morning light filtering through closed curtains.

If you are far more used to rude awakenings, in which your toddlers climb mercilessly into bed beside you – or between you and your partner – at five in the morning, or your alarm invariably jars your sensitive sleepiness with raucous cries that another day has arrived, then at least try to remember what it used to feel like to wake slowly and naturally. And, if you are determined to profit from the huge benefits of the art of relaxation, here and now determine that your mornings, at least once or twice a week, will be closer to the 'real thing'.

Autogenics

Autogenic training is related to the older art and therapy of hypnotism, and basically consists of a 'series of easy mental exercises designed to switch off the stress 'fight or flight' system of the body, and switch on the rest, relaxation and recreation system'. The basic premise is, that while preparation for emergency action is invaluable in a situation that *really* warrants it, the type of continuous stress we encounter in today's typical Western lifestyle often keeps us in a tense state of emergency preparation without real need.

Hence we tense our muscles, brace ourselves against unknown enemies, and maintain a state of readiness for fight or flight. Unlike the 'real' horrors that threatened our lives in olden times, however, we are more likely to be dealing with stress problems such as tax demands, mortgage applications and divorce, than with invading swamp monsters, marauding tribes or stampeding herds of half-wild horses or cattle. For this reason, our fight or flight reactions cannot be given full rein.

In fact we may not even be aware of the real cause of our tension and anxiety. As a result, the prolonged effects of the 'fight or flight' stimuli become translated into symptoms, of illness. Clenched muscles become cramped and painful, the constant tendency to evacuate the bowels or empty the bladder is misconstrued as diarrhoea or cystitis, and a rise in the rate of heartbeats is diagnosed as 'palpitations' or 'tachycardia of unknown origin'.

Autogenics as an art was developed by an eminent German neurologist earlier this century named Johannes Schultz[13]. He had studied yoga and hypnosis and as a result developed a method of mind training that influenced the body by means of exercises. He realised that if patients could be taught autohypnotic procedures, then they could feel more or less whatever simple sense impressions they were designed to feel, in their limbs or elsewhere.

In other words, Schultz felt that if patients repeated to themselves under specified conditions, autosuggestions such as: 'my left hand is warm', 'my right foot is cold', then they would actually experience the relevant physiological changes. It was, however, one of his pupils, Wolfgang Luthe, working in Canada, who wrote books on the topic and provided courses in it.

Method Basically, autogenic training consists of getting into a comfortable position, such as on an armchair or sofa, where you are unlikely to be distracted. The aim in view is the achievement of a state of mind called 'passive concentration', at which useful suggestions are most likely to take effect. There are six basic exercises, one example of which is imagining that your arms are heavy. Another, is imagining that your forehead is cool. You have to repeat the instruction to yourself three times.

When you are in a state as near to total relaxation as it is possible to achieve (called passive concentration), you are then free to make a simple suggestion to yourself that will be of benefit to you in your everyday life. It may involve remaining calm in certain situations, or staying headache free in situations in which you usually find you develop one. After each sequence of exercises, you will be

13. Inglis, B. and West, R. The Alternative Health Guide, Michael Joseph, London, pages 178–81

instructed to open your eyes, clench your fists, bend your arms in towards your body, then thrust them outwards, yawning hugely as you do so.

Autogenics can be self taught or learned at home, from a book or cassette tape. The London Centre for Autogenic Training lists some of the commoner stress-related disorders it can help. These include chronic fatigue and insomnia, anxiety and 'nerve' attacks, circulatory disturbance, stress-related heart conditions, raised blood pressure and migraine.

Psychosomatic diseases autogenics can help include asthma and eating problems, chronic nervous skin complaints, certain allergies, persistent intestinal and digestive problems, writer's cramp and some speech problems.

Common stress factors

As we saw earlier in this book, a growing number of diseases are starting to be related by research to stress. Among the commonest, are various forms of cancer, infectious illnesses, and auto-immune diseases, and since our immune defences play such a major role in protecting us from these conditions, there is certainly every reason for the conviction that stress is a major inhibitory factor of immune defence mechanisms.

Autogenics (and other forms of relaxation, such as yoga and meditation) are excellent ways of coping with the effects of stress upon our bodies and minds. However, it might be useful to pick a couple of common stress factors, and provide a few basic ideas for dealing with them. It is always *far* more satisfactory in the long run, to remove the underlying cause or causes of severe stress than it is only to learn to cope with their harmful effects.

Marital problems   These figure high on the stress rate tables, and one marriage in every three in the UK ends in the divorce courts. It is impossible to give detailed advice about unsatisfactory relationships generally, since each situation is unique, and to treat it as anything less is to deny the very real agony of mind unhappy matches can bring. However, here are one or two guidelines.

Whether you are a dissatisfied and 'guilty' feeling partner of someone who, you acknowledge, does their level best to please you, or the seriously wronged partner of a deeply unhappy marriage, bear one thought in mind. When we marry or take on a permanent partner, then we intend, at least to start off with, that the liaison will last for life, and we owe it to our partners to make them as happy as we can. But having said that, *no-one* has the right to make us seriously unhappy in a more or less continuous fashion. And neither should we try to remain with a partner to whom we cause a tremendous amount of grief. Certainly, we should do everything to mend a bad situation. But no marriage or partner is worth having if we become permanently wretched as a result. Some marriages may well be made in heaven, but others are fashioned in hell.

Never think that you ought not to seek divorce because 'the wedding cost so much', you don't want to 'upset the family', and you 'might not be able to manage alone'. The first two considerations ought not to enter the picture when the happiness of two independent individuals is at stake. And of course you can manage alone. People *do*. You *could*. And children are, beyond doubt, better off living with one or other relatively contented parent, than with both parents who are continually fighting and scrapping.

Money worries Money worries are even more common than marital disharmony. One of the problems at present, with the current rate of inflation, and the high numbers of unemployed, is that it is extremely easy to overspend and not to know what on earth to do about it.

Round the corner are numerous sharks, dying to lend you money at a high interest rate, and trying to capture your attention with offers to 'halve your monthly outgoings' in one fell swoop. The swoop with which these birds of prey fall upon their victims can be disastrous unless you are extremely lucky and pick one of the trustworthy companies around that really *do* have your interests (as well as their own) at heart.

Interest is, however, the name of the game in the vast majority of instances, however, and rather than panic and opt for the services of the first one you see advertising in the local evening paper – try a bank instead. If you greet this suggestion with derisive laughter, remember that banks do not usually go out of business overnight (at least, not the major ones), and that they have a reputation to maintain.

Even if you have only a small sum with which to start a current account, and cannot see your way clear to saving any money in the foreseeable future, you are still better off making the acquaintance of (and friends with) your local bank manager. He will explain about the usefulness of 'budget accounts' and how they work, and be far more likely to lend a sympathetic ear than money-lending companies who want their interest payments . . . or else.

Yoga

Yoga is another means of learning how to relax. Most yoga teachers introduce an element of mental and spiritual relaxation into their classes, as the original aim of yoga was to harmonise body, mind and spirit and make the vital force flow melodiously in harmony with the universe.

The exercises are of such a nature, in fact, that they demand that you move slowly and gracefully in order to do them properly. Meditation may or may not be included in your yoga class, but you are likely to find that simply by performing the exercises your thoughts slow and your mind becomes more tranquil. If a period of meditation *is* included in a yoga class you choose to join, then this is a definite bonus. You will be learning a technique that has proved highly beneficial in numerous ways to people suffering from many different varieties of physical, mental and spiritual problems.

POSITIVE THINKING

If admonitions to 'think positively' sound like a final resort when all else has failed, consider the following. Doctors and therapists have noticed for many years that patients who think they will recover, do so very much more quickly as well as more often, than those who remain pessimistic. More attention has been paid recently by health professionals of all kinds to the undoubted benefits of keeping patients cheerful.

We saw in an earlier chapter, how awareness of patients' psychological and spiritual needs is expressing itself in the recently developed diversional therapy for cancer patients. Remaining active, cheerful and forward looking is an attitude of mind greatly encouraged in England by the Bristol centre for cancer treatment, where a wide variety of natural, drug-free methods – including visualisation and meditation – are used to help patients either beat cancer altogether, or to remain as active and cheerful as possible during the final stages of their illness.

LAUGHTER THERAPY

Since positive thinking indisputably achieves results, although this is almost impossible to quantify in the scientific sense, it remains a fact that the positive thought processes themselves must have some kind of biochemical effect upon the sick tissue cells[14].

The effects of laughter have aroused much research interest over the past few years. Laughter has long been called 'the best medicine' and the saying seems to have been rooted in an instinctive awareness of the mechanism's benefits to health. Scientists in France, America and Canada are now becoming aware of what actually happens within the body when a person laughs.

Dr Pierre Vachet, a French researcher, reveals that laughter deepens the breath (again, the importance of oxygen!), expands blood vessels, improves the circulation, speeds tissue healing and stabilises many vital metabolic functions. It acts in fact like a powerful drug, but has no adverse side-effects.

Laughter also stimulates the secretion of beta-endorphins, natural painkillers made by brain cells, increases oxygenation of the tissues generally, and peps up the digestive processes. It has even been dubbed 'stationary jogging' as the biochemical effects are so similar. The research has lead to a new form of therapy in France, where it is known as 'jovialisme'. A jovialist is someone – a sort of therapeutic comedian – who gets paid for making sick people laugh.

In his book *Anatomy of an Illness*, a United States journalist described how he cured himself completely of ankylosing spondilitis, a painful auto-immune disease in which the backbone gradually fuses and becomes ramrod stiff. The method he adopted was to abandon all drugs, and to use megadoses of vitamin C, a healthier diet, and to watch hour upon hour of comedy films. Ten minutes of irrepressible laughter, he found, acted directly as an anaesthetic, and switched off the pain for two hours at a time.

Humour therapy is fast becoming accepted by orthodox doctors

14. Hodgkinson, Liz: Report in 'Alive' section, *Mail on Sunday*, London

in the USA, and some hospitals now have laughter rooms where patients go simply to roar with laughter. A Yugoslav writer, Branko Bokun, now living in the UK, has researched the therapeutic benefits of laughter for many years. In his book *Humour Therapy* (published by Vita Books) he suggests that it can effectively treat cancer, sex problems, psychosomatic illnesses and mental disorders. He believes that much modern illness is caused by stress, and that fear and worry and pent-up feelings cause the release of large amounts of the stress hormone adrenaline into the body.

If there is no outlet for the adrenaline (as we saw earlier, no physical battles to fight, no tangible enemies from whom to flee) then the adrenaline gradually erodes resistance to disease and to infections. It has adverse effects upon the heart and blood vessels and blood pressure, and particularly upon the immune defence system. Laughter is the best antidote, because it releases pent-up tension and calms the bodily systems down. In particular, it stops the over-secretion of adrenaline by the adrenal glands.

9 Natural Medicine

In the final chapter of this book, it seems a good idea to show what can be done to treat infectious illness when it does arise, in ways that least compromise the strength of the immune defence system.

It is important to reiterate here that in many instances orthodox treatment of infectious illnesses is mandatory. Fulminating septicaemia, cellulitis (soft tissue infection), chest and kidney infections, contaminated wounds, tuberculosis and osteomyelitis (infection of the bone marrow) are just a small, representative number of the cases where antibiotic treatment is vital. Many less serious conditions could also be cited (bacterial throat infections and tonsillitis, middle ear infections, bacterial conjunctivitis), in which the indication for antibiotic treatment would be equally strong.

Having said that, the aim of this book is to explain how hopefully to obviate the need for antibiotic drugs by so strengthening the immune defence system's resistance that the vast majority of bacterial and viral invasions are a complete failure on behalf of the pathogens. There is no reason why incipient and minor infections should not be treated with natural remedies alone, nor why the holistic approach should not be combined with orthodox treatment whenever this has to be used. Examples of natural remedies for several common infections will be given towards the end of this chapter.

HOMOEOPATHY AND VACCINATION

We explored the implications of vaccination as a protective technique against infections in Chapter 2. Not only is it safer and more rational to reinforce the individual's immune defences, but the process of vaccination necessarily involves introducing into the body, toxins that may place a considerable strain upon the resistance mechanisms as a whole.

Where the vaccinations are few and far between, the individual in the peak of condition and the risks of infection dire, then little harm is likely to ensue. Nevertheless, the very fact that doctors are never keen to vaccinate either children or adults suffering from infections, even minor ones like headcolds and sore throats, indicates the inadvisability of overtaxing the defence mechanisms in general and the immune response in particular.

However prophylactic the injected vaccine is intended to be, our bodies react to it as to a major pathogenic or chemical insult. Every tactic is brought to bear upon the threatening 'invader', and this must (just like digestive leucocytosis) weaken our ability to cope with other chemical, viral or bacteriological threats that may coincide.

Homoeopathic vaccination methods exist, by which the immune response is still evoked but with far less overall insult to the body's protective mechanisms. Before understanding how these work, it is necessary to explain a little of the precepts underlying homoepathy as a form of medical treatment.

Homoeopathy
The principle underlying homoepathy is the old-established maxim that 'like cures like'. This means that the medication chosen for a patient would, if given in allopathic concentrations, ie, in so many milligrams or millilitres, produce those very same symptoms of which the patient is complaining. (In some cases, such as the use of lead, mercury, cadmium, arsenic, belladonna, the effects would be fatal). The secret underlying homoeopathic medication, is that if it is *given in minute quantities*, a cure can be effected.

Homoeopathy (derived from the Greek 'homoios', meaning 'the same', and 'pathos' meaning 'suffering') dates back to the late eighteenth and early nineteenth centuries. Its founder, the German physician and chemist Dr Samuel Hahnemann, criticised the orthodox medicine he practised himself, on the grounds that it treated symptoms only and that, in many cases, the means it employed were harsh and injurious.

The administration of potent purges, stimulants and sedatives were popular current treatment methods, as was bleeding. Operations were performed without the benefits of anaesthetic or rudimentary hygiene measures, and Hahnemann looked at other possible therapeutic approaches. He shared, with naturopathic practitioners, the conviction that the body was essentially able to heal itself – provided its natural healing powers were not weakened or harmed in any way. And he viewed disease symptoms, not as signs of the disease itself, but as evidence of the body's reactions to the disease.

Hahnemann originally made this important deduction in 1790 from his observations of the effects of quinine upon himself when well. This drug was a known antidote to malaria, and was used in treating people such as missionaries who brought it back to this country from their journeys overseas. When he took quinine, though, he reacted with the same symptoms as an actual malaria sufferer. This, he became convinced, was evidence that symptoms were healthy reactions against pathological processes, to be encouraged rather than suppressed. He therefore spent the next twenty years experimenting both upon himself and upon volunteers. His findings were summed up in his book *Organum of Rational Healing*, which was published in 1810.

In later editions of the *Organum*, Hahnemann discussed the body's 'vital force' which had a great deal in common with the naturopathic view of the explanation of self-healing. He said, also, that it was this force which gave rise to the body's immune system. Along similar lines, he also viewed ill-health as the result of imbalance of the vital force, and identified the latter, too, with the 'Ch'i' of acupuncture. He viewed the point of treatment as the restoration of harmony to the body's vital force, and eschewed any approach which seemed to treat symptoms instead of aiming at relieving the underlying problem of imbalance.

During his years of experimental research, Samuel Hahnemann experimented with a wide range of substances in many varying degrees of dilution. He was able to confirm, again and again, that 'like cures like', and also discovered that diluting a chemical substance by shaking it up in water or other solvent (a method he referred to as 'succussion'), in fact increased that substance's potency rather than weakening it. In other words, the smaller the dose, the more powerful the effect.

Hahnemann's successes made him very unpopular with both doctors and apothecaries. A court in Austria forbade him to practise and for a time he returned as lecturer in medicine to the University of Leipzig. However, his fame was secured by his successful treatment of the Prince Schwarzenburg and again in 1831, when his methods were far more successful in treating victims of a European cholera epidemic than were conventional methods. He practised in Paris for a time, and died, famous, in 1843.

When homoeopathic remedies are prepared nowadays, 'mother tinctures' (crude alcoholic extracts of the plant or other material used) are made and diluted a hundredfold. The first hundredth dilution is termed 1C; the next, 2C, is a hundredth dilution of the 1C preparation, that is, ten thousand times the dilution of the original tincture. This dilution process is known as 'trituration'. The preparation is then shaken vigorously by hand or machine many times over, the process being known as 'potentisation'.

Explaining how diluting a remedy can possibly increase its potency has proved a major problem. Theories exist that the secret lies in the molecular energies of the active compounds, which increase during the grinding and succussing stages. The preparation finally given to the patient is a very low concentration of the substance in a state of high energy.

The potency of homoeopathic preparations normally on sale in chemists and health food shops is 6C. It is not considered to be safe to make higher potencies available for self-medication. Qualified homoeopaths always advise patients with all but trivial problems to seek a professional consultation rather than to rely on self-medication which, on the whole, they do not consider to be satisfactory. The skill of the experienced practitioner lies in taking a very detailed case history from the patient and noting certain points of observation about his appearance, voice and so on, and then matching the patient to the homoeopathic preparation that is right for him or her as an individual.

Vaccination

The internationally famous Greek homoeopath, George Vithoulkas, is of the opinion that orthodox vaccination in certain susceptible people can weaken and distort the vital force, sometimes irreparably. He is convinced that the infectious illnesses against which babies and children are routinely vaccinated, will only occur in those who are susceptible to them, and prove dangerous only in those with a weakened vital force, secondary either to constitutional factors (for instance, the prenatal causes indicated by naturopaths) or to orthodox treatment methods. Instead of vaccinating children, Dr Vithoulkas opts for treating them constitutionally with homoeopathic remedies, since these strengthen, rather than impair, the body's immune and other defences.

Should they develop measles or mumps for instance despite these measures, then they should be treated with homoeopathic, not allopathic, remedies. Vithoulkas goes so far as to say that, in his own experience, it seems likely that certain diseases, especially those with an autoimmune aetiology such as rheumatoid arthritis and multiple sclerosis, probably resulted in the first place from earlier vaccination. He believes that the increased incidence of autoimmune diseases and the existence of AIDS may well be due to this, too. Other major causes of serious diseases, he feels, include other forms of allopathic suppression, including the use of antibiotics, major tranquillisers, and steroid drugs.

He claims that vaccinating children damages their immune defence mechanisms and makes them more prone to other disorders such as sore throats, colds, chest infections and middle ear infections. This state of affairs can, it seems, be treated homoeopathically, but the form the treatment taken does remove the protection against specific infectious illnesses against which the children have been vaccinated[15].

George Vithoulkas is not in fact in favour of attempting to immunise using homoepathic potencies of vaccines. The reason for this, he believes, is that, in order to produce a protective influence by giving the remedy, one would have to make the patient ill. However, many homoeopathic practitioners *are* in favour of the practice, and treat appropriate patients with them.

---

15. Lockie. Andrew: 'Miasms and vaccines: the Vithoulkas view' *Journal of Alternative Medicine* (January 1985) page 8

OTHER FORMS OF TREATMENT FOR NATURAL VITALITY

Two forms of alternative medicine which should be mentioned in the context of treating infectious illnesses without harming our natural resistance, include biochemic tissue salts, and herbal medicine. Both are based upon holistic principles, and enhance our vitality and natural vigour, correcting imbalance where this exists. Biochemic tissue salts are invariably compatible with orthodox medicines as are most home herbal remedies. If in doubt, you can always check with a qualified herbalist or your pharmacist.

BIOCHEMIC TISSUE SALTS

Biochemic tissue salts were the brainchild of a German homoeopathic physician, Dr W. H. Schuessler, during the 1870s. He felt there to exist a possible link between diseases and an imbalance or deficiency of essential minerals. His basic approach can be summed up as follows:

• the human body contains twelve essential mineral salts, which have to be balanced for the cells of the body to function properly (ie, for health to exist)
• even slight disturbances in this balance, can cause illnesses
• the normal balance of these tissue salts can be restored by taking the appropriate mineral salts (now known as biochemic tissue salts).

Naturopaths and other alternative therapists often recommend salts to be taken – they are available in many chemists in the UK now. They are prepared in homoeopathic concentrations and are absolutely safe to take. Here are some examples of common infective symptoms and the salts that prove useful in their treatment.

Fever The first remedy in all types of fever is Ferrum Phos., which effectively treats a rapid pulse, flushed face, and shivery feeling. This can be alternated with other salts as indicated, ie, for second stage of fever, when the tongue is coated and there may be constipation – Kali Mur.; fever associated with weakness and nerviness – Kali Phos.; evening rise in temperature, with hot dry skin

– Kali Sulph.; for early stage of fever, when there is excessive thirst, unrelieved by water, and dry skin – Natrum Mur. Dose: four tablets every half hour, less frequently as fever subsides.

Swollen glands   For soft, tender glands, especially in the neck and throat – Kali Mur; for the fever and pain in acutely swollen glands, Ferrum Phos.; for swelling of glands, if hard – Calcarea Fluor.; for swollen glands, inclined to suppurate – Silicea (alternate with Calcarea Phos.). Dose: four tablets every two hours.

Headcolds   For early stages, dryness of nose, headache, fever – Ferrum Phos., alternate with Kali Mur. For the cold when fully developed, with thick white secretions and coated tongue – Kali Mur., alternating with Ferrum Phos. When there is a clear, frothy, watery discharge, with stinging inside nose, sneezing, loss of sense of smell and cold blisters on lip – Natrum Mur.. For dry skin, fever – to promote perspiration, and for heavy discharge of greenish-yellow mucus – Kali Sulph.. During early sore throat stage, Calcarea Sulph. will often prevent a cold from developing.

Earache   When inflammatory symptoms are present, fever, throbbing etc – Ferrum Phos.; when earache is accompanied by thin, yellow discharge, sharp pains under ear – Kali Sulph.; foul matter discharged from the ear – Silicea; earache with sharp neuralgic pains in or around the ear – Magnesia Phos.

Herbal medicine

Although herbal remedies are available for self-treatment, and some herbalists prescribe herbal medication for the relief of symptoms, qualified herbalists do not regard this as the true practice of herbal medicine in the holistic sense. They aim at the harmonising of an unbalanced life force by the use of whole plants taken from their natural state, and while it is safe to take herbal patent medicines prepared by reputable companies, it is always better to consult a qualified practitioner. He or she will be able to assess *why* your resistance to infection has been lowered, and the best way of restoring the protective strength of your immune mechanisms.

   Here are examples of home remedies for infective symptoms.

Headcolds 2 teaspoons organic cider vinegar in a quarter-litre (half-pint) tumbler of cold or warm water, drunk morning and evening.

Irritating coughs These can be helped by the same remedy as above, using twice the quantity of cider vinegar. A gram of natural vitamin C taken every three hours as well is helpful, as is the addition of two teaspoons of honey if the treatment as it stands is not effective.

Sore throats A special gargle[16]

285ml (10fl oz) cider vinegar
115g   (4oz) honey
 30g   (1oz) red sage (garden sage, *Salvia officinalis*)
 15g   (½oz) self-heal (*Prunella vulgaris*)

Heat cider vinegar with herbs until very hot but not boiling, in a non-aluminium pan. Allow to cool, strain after twenty-four hours, add honey, stir until dissolved, bottle and cap securely. Use two teaspoons in half a glass of warm water and gargle thrice daily.

Boils and Abscesses To draw either to a head, either half a raw lemon bound to the spot, or half a baked fresh onion, applied as hot as is tolerable. When the boil or abscess comes to a head and bursts, provided it is mild and you are not generally unwell with it, start a course of Echinacea, a very useful plant antibiotic and powerful blood cleanser[17]. Potter's, Baldwin's and Gerard House all sell Echinacea tablets.

Conjunctivitis Either of these makes a good eye bath, for infected eyes, that have inflamed whites and ooze yellow or whitish pus:

A teaspoon of fennel seeds, crushed, steeped and covered for twenty minutes in a cup of boiling water. Strain and cool. Bathe eye(s) three to four times daily.

A tablespoon of elder flowers, boiled for five minutes in a cupful of water, left to infuse for ten minutes and then strained.

16. Hanssen, M. *Hanssen's Complete Cider Vinegar* Thorsons Publishers, Wellingborough, UK, pages 45–6
17. Griggs, B. *The Home Herbal* Pan Books, London, pages 35–6

Index

144 · Index